Battlefields Bibles and Bandages

Portraying an American Civil War Nun

Kelsey Jones

aka: Mother Mary Elizabeth, S. S. B.

HERITAGE BOOKS
2005

HERITAGE BOOKS

AN IMPRINT OF HERITAGE BOOKS, INC.

Books, CDs, and more—Worldwide

For our listing of thousands of titles see our website
at
www.HeritageBooks.com

Published 2005 by
HERITAGE BOOKS, INC.
Publishing Division
65 East Main Street
Westminster, Maryland 21157-5026

International Standard Book Number: 0-7884-3582-5

In Memory of Jack Jones
-without whom this book would never have been written.
And to Mary Virginia Kimmell
- who was an inspiration to me in the re-enacting community.

Acknowledgements

Heartfelt thanks to Sister Maria Elena, O. S. F., and all of the Sisters from all the Orders that have helped with the research involved in this book and in perfecting my own persona, and have show so much enthusiasm for this book and given selflessly of their time to help.

To The Kimmells for their love and support and for teaching me that change is inevitable and that what you make of it depends on what you put into it.

A special thank you to the surgeons of the U.S. 16th Iowa for their support and for urging me to finish this book during a time that was so difficult for me.

And the warmest thank you goes to my late husband for the love and support he gave me while I was writing this book. We all will miss him very much.

-Kelsey

To My newest initiate

Sr. Mary Virginia

In Gods Love!

Mother Mary Elizabeth O.S.B.

Foreword

In April 1997 Jack asked me to go with him to a Civil War reenactment as a participant instead of an on-looker. I was excited and scared. I wasn't sure how I would be accepted as a greenhorn.

As luck would have it the first reenactment of the season was at Keokuk, Iowa. There I met the second moving force in my life (Jack being the first), Mary Virginia Kimmell (affectionately known as MV by all and sundry).

She welcomed me with open arms, as did her husband and the other members of the Missouri Brigade Medical Service. They showed me how much fun a reenactment can be and how to make it more enjoyable for visitors as well.

We were asked to join the group as permanent members. I can still remember my excitement on hearing this news. Then I found out that their nurses were all supposed to be Nuns! I didn't know anything about being a Nun. In fact, I wasn't even Catholic!

I began the seemingly monumental task of looking for information, only to find there wasn't very much readily available on Nuns and their role during the Civil War. The harder I looked the more disappointed I became.

Finally, someone put me in touch with Sister Maria Elena of the Sisters of the Third Order of St. Francis, in East Peoria, Illinois. She was so excited to hear from me and very willing to help me with the information I needed. As the Historian of the East Peoria Motherhouse she also was able to loan me pieces of habits they wore during the Victorian Era and I was able to make exact duplication of them.

Even then, information was skimpy at first. As my searches grew wider I began getting information from Catholic Parishes that led me to other places to look. I heard about other books that talked about Nuns or had photos of Civil War Era Nuns in them. Finally I was getting somewhere.

What has taken me six years to gather and put together here, is information I wish I had when I first began my impression of a Civil War Era Nun. Hopefully this will be of great help to those who are considering this fun and rewarding persona. There are now many books readily available to help with your research, This one is just the beginning.

In addition to research on how to portray a Nun, I also had to research Civil War medicine in general. Copying antiquated nursing and surgical techniques and figuring out how to prepare realistic looking wounds has taken much of my time and energy of late.

A friend of mine recently asked me why I wanted to write a book on this subject. What passion would be so strong to work this hard to put forth this type of information?

I had to stop and think about it before I could answer her. For the fire was not a sudden need to write about this subject, but grew more slowly. The more I learned, the more I wanted to know. The more I knew, the more I wanted to share with others about these women and the things they did for Christianity in particular and for the populace as a whole. It is their dedication and passion that has fueled this fire and continues to fuel it with every line I write.

Please remember this not the last word on Nun impressions. These are only my views and information I have researched. There were many different Orders of Sisters and as many different views of the way they did things as there are women in the Sisterhood.

Relax and enjoy yourself. Do the research and attempt to do it right. That is all they and I ask.

(Illustration Reference 2)

Pope Pius IX   1846—1878

Born in Senigallia, Italy in 1792 with the name of Giovanni Maria, he was of delicate physical constitution. He devoted his life to religious studies and was ordained priest in 1819. He was known to have been an eloquent preacher, prompt in charity toward everyone, zealous for the supernatural as well as the material well-being of his Diocese, devoted to his Clergy and all but firm in his principles. He received his Cardinal's hat in 1840 at the age of 48. On the evening of 16 June 1846 he was elected Pope and became Pius IX. His was a difficult pontificate, but "because of that he was a great Pope". On 7 February 1878 the longest pontificate in history ended with his holy death.

Chapter 1

The History of Women Religious

In order to portray a role accurately, a study must be undertaken of the history of that role. In this chapter you will find a brief history of the Women Religious in the Catholic Church from its very beginning, ending with the Civil War period. The history has been condensed for the sake of brevity in this book. Consult the bibliography for a listing of books if you are interested in more of the history of the Catholic Sisterhoods or the Catholic Church.

Monasticism during the time between A.D. 500 and A.D. 1500 exhibits phases of vital significance for the mental and moral growth of Western Europe. Although both the aims and the tone of life of the members of the different religious orders varied, monasticism generally favored tendencies which were among the most peaceful and progressive of the middle ages. For women especially the convent fostered some of the best sides of intellectual, moral and emotional life. It was for several centuries a determining factor in regard to women's economical status. There is a growing consciousness today of the debt of gratitude which mankind as a whole owes to the monastic and religious orders.

The fact that these women appeared in a totally different light to their contemporaries is generally overlooked; that the Monk and the Nun enjoyed the esteem and regard of the general public throughout a term of almost a thousand years is frequently forgotten. Even at the time of the Reformation, when religious contentions were at their height, the Nun who was expelled from her home appeared deserving of pityrather than of reproach to her more enlightened contemporaries. As a part of an institution that had outlived its purpose she was perhaps bound to pass away. But the work she had done and the aims for which she had striven contributed their share in formulating the new standards of life. The attitude of mind, which had been harbored and cultivated in the cloister, must be reckoned among the most civilizing influences, which have helped to develop mental and moral strength in Western Europe.

The right to self-development and social responsibility which the woman of today so persistently asks for, is in many ways comparable to the right which the convent secured to womankind well over a thousand years ago. The woman of today, who realizes that the home circle often affords insufficient scope for her energies, had a precursor in the nun who sought a field of activity in the convent. For the nun also hesitated to undertake the customary duties and accept the ordinary joys of life. While this hesitation may be attributed to distortion of instinct, it can hardly, in the case of the nun, be attributed to weakness of character. She chose a path in life which was neither smooth nor easy, and in this path she accomplished great things, many of which still have living value.

The social value of cloistered life in itself has often been disputed. A profession, which involved estrangement from family ties, appeared altogether harmful to the Protestant of the 16th century. Moreover, monasteries and religious houses were bound up in the reformer's mind with the supremacy of Rome from which he was striving hard to shake himself free. Wherever the breach with Rome had effected the old settlements, they were dissolved and their inmates were thrust back into civic life. To men this meant much, but it meant even more to women. In losing the possibility of religious profession at the beginning of the 16th century, women lost the last chance that remained to them of an activity outside the home circle. The subjection of women to a round of domestic duties became more complete when nunneries were dissolved, and marriage for generations afterwards was women's only recognized vocation.

Historical Beginings

The Mother Age (Pre 400 AD) period is generally looked upon as an advance from an earlier stage of savagery, and considered to be a part of the beginnings of settled tribal life. It brought with it the practice of tillage and agriculture, and led to the domestication of some of the smaller animals and the invention of weaving and spinning, achievements with which it is recognized that women must be credited.

During the times of declining heathendom the drift of society had been toward curtailing woman's liberty of movement and interfering with her freedom of action. When Europe crossed the threshold of history the characteristics of the father-age were already in the ascendant; the social era, when the growing desire for certainty of fatherhood caused individual women and their offspring to be brought into the possession of individual men, had already begun. The influence of women was more and more restricted owing to their domestic subjection. But traditions of a time when it had been otherwise still lingered.

The Father-age (approximately 450 AD) succeeding to the Mother-age in time altogether revolutionized the relations of the sexes; transient sex unions, formerly the rule, were gradually eliminated by capture and retention of wives from outside the tribal group. The change marks a distinct stop in social advance. When men as heads of families succeeded to much of the influence women had held in the tribe, barbarous tendencies were checked and a higher moral standard was attained. But, this was done at the cost of her prerogative, and her social influence to some extent passed from her.

When contact with Christianity brought with it the possibility of monastic settlements, the love of domestic life had not penetrated so deeply, nor was its conditions so uniformly favorable, but that many women were ready to break away from it. Reminiscences of an independence belonging to them in the past, coupled with the desire of leadership, made many women loathe to conform to life inside the family as wives and mothers under conditions formulated by men. Tendencies surviving from the earlier period, and still un-subdued, made the advantages of married life weigh light in the balance against a loss of liberty. To conceive the force of these tendencies is to gain an insight into the elements the convent directly absorbs.

But in the convent the influence of womankind lasted longer. Spirited nuns and independent-minded abbesses turn to view the possibilities open to them in a way which commands respect and repeatedly secures superstitious reverence in the outside world. The influence and the powers exerted by these women are altogether remarkable, especially during early Christian times. We also come across frequent instances of lawlessness among the women who band together in the convent[1]. That very love of independence, when coupled with self-control and consciousness of greater responsibility led to beneficial results. This was lost when it was accompanied by the hatred for every kind of restraint.

Different ages have different standards of purity and faithfulness. The loose or unattached women of the past are of many kinds and many types. To apply the term prostitute to them raises a false idea of their position as compared with that of women in other walks of life. To deal with them as a class we must realize that the only commonality they had was the indifference to the ties of family, and that the men who associate with them were not held responsible for them or toward their offspring.

We should bear in mind the part these women have played and the modifications which their status has undergone clearly affects monasticism. The convent accepted the dislike the women felt to domestic subjection and blessed them in their refusal to undertake the duties of married life. It offered an escape from the tyranny of the family, but it did so on condition of a sacrifice of personal independence, as the condition in the outside world more and more involved the loss of good repute. A greater contrast than that of the loose woman and the nun is hard to conceive and yet they have in common that they are both the outcome of

---

[1] Eckenstein, *Women Under Monasticism*, Dugdale, *Monasticon*, 'Chatteris' Vol. 2

the refusal among womankind to accept married relations on the basis of the subjection imposed by the Father-age.

Convent Beginnings

Prior to the 6th Century A. D., women who devoted their life to religion lived in the home of their father. They wore a simple veil and spent their time engrossed in study and to works of piety that was considered proper for the genteel women of the period. Their dress differed little from that of their lay sisters and only a simple veil separated them from the rest of society. They renounced offers of marriage and sought "protection" from the church officials. During this period this meant a letter from the local pastor or from the reigning pope. Even with the "protection" of the church in hand, it meant little if the woman's father chose to marry her to someone for the political or financial gain that it would bring to the family. So these "letters" were upheld only if the father chose to do so.

At the beginning of the 6th century, Caesarius, bishop of Arles, had persuaded his sister Caesaria to join him at Arles and preside over the women who had gathered there to live and work under his guidance. While this was by no means the very first convent established it was the first convent recorded to have brought together a number of women under a single rule.

Caesarius now created a rule of life for his sister and those women whom she was prepared to direct. He arranged it according to the teaching of the "Fathers of the Church". He goes on to stipulate that those who join the Community (either as maidens or widows) should enter once and for all and renounce all claims to outside property. The community accepted only those who came of their own accord, accepted the routine and were prepared to live on the terms of strictest equality without property or servants of their own.

Children under six years of age were not to be accepted at all, nor were the daughters of noble parents, or lowly-born girls be taken in readily to be brought up and educated. This injunction shows how the religious at this period wished to keep the advantages of artistic and intellectual training within their own community. They had no desire for the spread of education outside of their convent walls as those communities of later formation were so well known for.

Considerable time and thought were devoted to the practice of chants and to choir-singing so as to better celebrate God. Following Celtic usage, the chant was taken up in turn by relays of the professed, who kept up the chant night and day all year round in a perpetual praise of Divinity. The great debt owed by the art of music to the enthusiasm of these early singers is often overlooked.

Reading and writing were practiced in classes by these women, not only in Arles, but in many of the communities of the period. Domestic occupations, such as cooking and cleaning were performed in turns. The women also spun wool and wove it into cloth to make their own garments and they practiced the art of weaving fine pictoral church hangings.

There were further injunctions about tending the infirm and healing practices. Stern advice about the hatefulness of quarrels and the proper behavior that benefited the community as a whole and the individual nun in particular was included in the rule.

In the year 506, at the Synod of Agde, it was decreed that no nun however good in character should receive the veil (to be permanently bound by a vow) before her fortieth year. This along with the rule set upon the communities created a sober and serious spirit for these early settlements.

It was part of the plan to secure independence for the communities that Caesarius had founded by asking the Pope's protection for his monasteries, one of which was for men and one for women, against possible interference from the outside. He also begged that the Pope would confirm the grants of property, which had already been made to these establishments and the power of the Bishop in regard to the settlements should be limited to visitation. Other communities then began to request copies of and establish this same rule within their own houses and establishment of orderly communities became more common.

It is evident that women readily accepted life on the conditions proffered and were content to be controlled and protected by these men, or at least found it preferable to the prison like atmosphere that marriage had become. The loss of personal freedom was felt to be at a much lesser degree in these communities than in the bonds of matrimony. It was only when the untamed German element with its craving for self-assertion came in, that difficulties between the bishops and heads of nunneries arose. It is obvious that at this point religious life within these Communities must then have suffered an upheaval that was to last for many years.

It was late in the 6th century when the nuns began to revolt against the chafing of men's rule. Already by this time difficulties had begun to arise. Monarchs who had placed daughters in the nunneries then recanted and asked that they should leave to be married. It had become increasingly difficult for abbesses to maintain discipline within their communities.

The Years Following 630 A. D.

During this period a great portion of the women who founded religious houses were members of ruling families. It was not unusual for a princess to receive a grant of land from her husband on the occasion of her marriage, and this land together with what she inherited from her father she could dispose of at will. She often devoted this property to founding a religious house where she established her daughters, and to which she retired either during her husband's lifetime or after his death. Although it was not unheard of, they usually did not rule as abbess in the religious settlements they founded. Rather, an abbess was appointed by them and recognized by a prelate.

The great honor paid by Christianity to the celibate life and the wide fields of action open to a princess in a religious house were strong inducements to the sisters and daughters of kings to take the veil. It was Wilfrith[2]—who was a prelate sometime before 670, who advocated the principle that a queen could choose to leave her husband and retire to a religious settlement and that such a decision would secure her the favor of the church. The husband who found himself bereft of a wife did not always take this lightly. There were times that this behavior would cause rifts between the monarch and the church.

The marriage of a Christian princess was made an occasion for extending the faith as an ecclesiastic usually accompanied her to her new household. This was proven to be the rule many times during the next few centuries as the story of conversion repeated itself over and over again. Well over 30 centers of religious study were established during this period. Here we find high-born and influential women as abbesses and the head of establishments, which were centers of contemporary culture. This enabled the previously barbarian Anglo Saxons to attain a high degree of culture within 100 years of their conversion.

Through out these early years, however, these religious settlements depended on the temperament of the ruling princes and kings for their safety and property. When the prince was decadent, the seduction of the Nuns even within their own monastery was known to have occurred. Lands and building could and would be snatched out of the hands of Bishops, Abbesses and Abbots. The religious centers were powerless to prevent the terrorizing of their communities and written censures from the church had no affect.

Beyond 800 A.D.

By 800 A.D. the Convent was a place of residence and a training school for women of the ruling class. Girls came to be educated and either became a permanent member or left to be married. Widows often returned to the monastic life desirous of solitude and study. During the 10th and 11th centuries, some of the convents gained additional importance because of their close connection with political affairs and interests of the time.

---

[2] Wilfrith – Bishop Wilfrith held this office fromapprox 660 to 685 AD

It is interesting to note here some of the general occupations and productive capacities of the nuns during the early Christian times. This work included art production of every kind (weaving, embroidery, painting and illuminating) as well as writing (during this period it was considered an art form.

From the very beginnings of monastic life the idea that idleness is the root of all evil propelled the well ordered communities to fix times for work and for leisure, for eating, sleeping and for attending divine service and were enforced by routine. The purpose of the ordinary settlement (beyond observing canonical hours) was to educate girls, to train Novices and to provide suitable occupation for the Nuns of the convent. In all houses reading and copying of books of devotions was included among the occupations.

Between the 8th and 14th centuries religious communities were the centers of production in handcrafts and in art industry. A sense of joint ownership united the members of each community and giving the convent inmate a sense that the house's possessions were in a sense her own. Increased communication with the south and east brought books, materials and other beautiful objects to copy and illustrate. A treasure house of designs and ornamentation were kept in the libraries of the convents. Bookbinding was commonly practiced in each of the houses as well as nursing and healing skills.

Nuns greatly distinguished themselves in weaving pictoral church hangings and embroidering altar cloths and church vestments. It is here that the techniques of each were brought to their highest perfection and apart from personal decoration the arts of weaving and embroidery were encouraged in every way. Gold and jewels were used on silk for especially rich church hangings. Gold fringe and cords were specially created for the church banners and hangings. The proficiency acquired by the girl in the convent was not lost if she returned to the world. Badges and standards worked by ladies at baronial courts during the age of romance was no doubt influenced by what had been evolved in church decoration. England took the lead in art industry during this time. Spinning, weaving, sewing and designing also reached new heights of excellence as well.

Miniature painting also grew to great heights in the communities during this period. Some of the work seems to have been copied from embroidery work as they often had a pattern or diagonal lines filling the background of these works. Some of the work is so tiny that one observer was wont to say that it would have been too tedious for me to create.

The art of herbal medicine and healing advanced during this period as well as the religious communities of both men and women began to establish healing centers for their communities. This skill translated well in the management skills required of chatelaines and mistresses of large holdings of the period.

Why Were Convents So Popular?

There were numerous reasons for the popularity of convent life. One reason stemmed from the political subjection of Saxons by Frankish rule. The nobleman who turned monk was freed from obligation thrust on him by the new regime. He became exempt from fighting under the standard of the conqueror and the property he bestowed upon the religious settlement was in a way withdrawn from the enemy.

However, when the Saxon people regained their independence they were quick to realize the advantages of close union of religion and state. The most powerful families often vied with each other in founding and endowing religious settlements. Settlements of women were rapidly gaining importance and often rivaled the episcopal sees in wealth and influence.

The monotony of life in the castles or burghs of this period can hardly be exaggerated. Means of communication were few and occasions for it rare. When master and men were absent, engaged in a private brawl or summoned to attend then duke or king weeks and months would go by without a reminder of the existence of the outside world. The arrival of a traveler offered welcome diversion. While the young nobleman followed his father and was rewarded with opportunities for education and widening his horizons through social intercourse, the young noble woman was isolated at home from every opportunity afforded her brother.

And so it is with the daughters of these families that the religious houses first found favor. These settlements offered companionship of equals and gave domestic and intellectual training, the best of it's kind. The word college was often applied to these settlements. They were endowed colleges were girls were received from the age of seven to be trained and women devoted to learning arts permanently resided. Responsibilities of married and unmarried life were undertake early in youth. Often they left at the age of 14 to be married and some even became abbesses at the age of 12! At this period of time however, many settlements did not take permanent vows.

The range of subjects taught in Saxon nunneries was wide. It included the study of religious and classical writers, spinning, weaving and embroidery. Not only was convent discipline taught, but also that of common law. It is interesting to note the large number of princesses of ruling dynasties that were unmarried and remained in convents. This suggests that it was prudent for the royal family to place their princesses in the convent in preference to contracting matrimonial alliances during this period. These settlements must have been congenial in more ways than one.

As Abbess they held a place of authority second to that of no woman in the land. Her land hold usually extended over a vast area. She had duties and privileges of a barron and had the right of ban, issued summons to appear in her court, and her proctor gave judgments. At times they even secure the right to strike their own coin! The abbesses were in direct contact with court and politics.

These so called free-abbeys were under the obligation of entertaining the king and his retinue in return for the privileges granted them,. The king had no fixed residence during this tie and often stayed at these religious centers during holy days.

However in the late part of the 11th century the popularity of the convent for women began to decline as the wife began to gain better position under Danish rule and the spread of the system of feudal tenure excluded women from holding property, which they could devote to the advantage of their sex. During the reign of William I of Normandy, many Benedictine houses for monks were founded or restored, but none for women.

From the 12th Century

The 12th century (the middle ages) has been named the golden age for monasticism. Prosperity of existing monasteries increased greatly and new monasteries and religious orders were established. A wave of enthusiasm, for the life of a religious settlement emanating from France swept over Western Europe. The cloister and court were seen as centers of civilized life. The monk and the nun gave new meaning to religious devotion by turning their activities into channels which first made possible the approximation of class-to-class equalization within these communities. The desire for religious life now penetrated into the lower strata of society and special attention was focused on women of the lower classes.

The movement of the 16th century commonly spoken of as the "Reformation" was the forcible manifestation of a revolution in thought, which had long been preparing and is characterized by a sense of assurance, aspiration and optimism. Among the important social changes affected by the Reformation, the dissolution of the monasteries forms a small but significant feature. This feature is pregnant with meaning if considered in the light of the changing standards of family and sexual morality. For those who attacked the Church of Tome in her fundamentals, while differing points of doctrine, were at one in the belief that the state of morality needed amendments and that marriage supplied the means of affecting the desired change.

During the Reformation Period Cardinal Wolsey[3] advocated the suppression of smaller monasteries for the purpose of founding and endowing seats of learning on a large scale soon after his accession to power. He was advanced to chancellorship in 1513 and was nominated cardinal by the Pope in 1515. The Nuns were removed to other places of religion and their property appropriated and added to his own holdings. While it is noted most of the communities dissolved had fewer than 12 members it roused considerable local dissatisfaction and brought censure on Woolsey from the king, Charels V[th]. The king's ire was further roused when the cardinal accepted an appointment of an abbess to a house, which was under royal patronage and where acceptance of the abbess belonged to the king. The unsuitability of the king's choice and the king's objection to the cardinal's choice led to the appointment of a third abbess. This led to the suspension of dissolution proceedings for the time being. Meanwhile, Woolsey was forced into retirement and died the following year.

In 1533 the Parliament had passed the act abolishing appeals of the Court of Rome, and among other rights had transferred the right of monastic visitation from the Pope to the king. The following year the king claimed to be recognized as the head of the Church. It was part of Henry's policy to bring about gradual changes that undermined prerogatives without making a decided break with the Church. Cromwell was appointed vice-regent in ecclesiastical matters. It was he who then deputized agents to visit religious houses and interrogate the monks and nuns concerning the property of their house, the number of its inmates and its founders and privileges, its maintenance of discipline and the right of conduct of its inmates. The agents then enjoined severance from the Pope or any any other foreign superior, and directed those who had taken the vow, whether men or women, henceforth to observe strict seclusion. A daily lesson in scripture was to be read; the celebration of the hours was to be curtailed. A further injunction that the professions made under the age of twenty-four was declared invalid thus further reducing the populace of the communities. The visitors added other special injunctions after viewing the place and nature of accounts. Houses that lived by raising animals fell into decay when the inmates were not allowed to leave to tend them.

It is this time in which the picture arises of the spirit of the Christian populace and the Catholic populace of today. The Roman Christians, craving the pomp and circumstance of ritual and refinement of union with Rome would become the Roman Catholics of today. While the Christians with their insistence on independence from Rome would become the widely varied Christian populace of today. As the hatred toward Rome grew and the struggle for power ensued, few communities were able to

---

[3] Eckenstein, *Women Under Monasticism*

withstand the hatred of the surrounding communities for what they considered heresy. The nuns were accused of sins and crimes from pulpits of the Lutheran Churches and this in turn fired the citizenry to attack convents both verbally and physically. At the close of the century then, we see the changing attitudes toward the Catholic Church that was to carry through to the 19th century.

Only 18 communities survived the terrorization. During the last years, the beleaguered women suffered harassment by Cromwell's officers, royal officials and by the students they put in place of absent or deposed abbesses. They lacked the community solidarity created by observance, which enabled many continental nuns to sustain an effective resistance. Henry VIIIth moved against them with the same fierce self-righteousness that drove his relationships with his wives.

Many of the English nuns came from insignificant families who could endow them modestly in neighborhood houses but could not defend their property against the combined forces of king and nobility. Eventually every house in England was closed and the nuns turned out without their dowries to seek shelter with their families or live as best they could on meager pensions. Henry distributed most of the monastic lands among his noble supporters. Lead was stripped from the roofs and fittings melted down with the bells. Relics and pictures were shipped to London for burning. Plate and jewels were also sent to London and dispersed. Furniture, utensils, and vestments were sold on the spot. The roofless and gutted buildings were left to decay.

Henry VIII wrote the "Six-Articles of 1539"[4] that declared it a felony to break a vow of chastity. Thus, of 10,000 former Nuns that lived in England after the suppression, none were allowed to marry. Hungry and abused, many Nuns held out in their decaying buildings until forced away and still lived to return under Mary Tudor.[5]

Into the 19th Century and the American Civil War

By the 19th century, women religious had been reinstated as part of the mainstream of religious society. The work they accepted, once again defined their roles as a necessary entity within the lay communities surrounding them. As they increased in number, so did their works, including education, charity work, nursing, caring for the elderly, orphanages, visiting mental facilities, prisons , work and pest houses, to name only a few.

Their new freedom from religious persecution made them widely popular during an age when women were redefining their roles in society. This increase in population made it possible for religious communities to

---

[4] Eckenstein, *Woman Under Monasticism*
[5] Eckenstein, *Woman Under Monasticism*

21

expand into missionary work in underdeveloped countries. The American Continents were considered such, and a great many communities sent groups of women religious to the Americas to found branches of their Orders and bring stability to Catholic communities in those regions.

Europe was developing rapidly in the field of medicine. Women religious worked side by side with doctors and took full advantage of medical and nursing colleges there. Europe continued to be at war on several home fronts giving the Sisters valuable hands on training in battlefield medicine. Thus when the missionary groups arrived in the United States they brought with them the training as nurses, hospital administrators and also knowledge of the newest medical techniques. They trained each new member of their Order as well. Indeed, many of the religious communities had rules of patient care written into their charters.

In the lay society, women were limited to nursing of their own families and were only familiar with folk remedies handed down through the maternal line. There were some exceptions where women grew up in physician's households and learned more of medicine than other lay women. Men, on the other hand, worked as orderlies in the hospitals, were charged with nursing duties and attended medical colleges. The first class of trained nurses graduated from Bellevue Hospital in 1872[6] – far too late to help during the Civil War.

The first shot of the Civil War (April 12, 1861) found the nursing sisters already working in the hospitals founded by the Catholic Church and in other areas noted earlier. As it became apparent the military was woefully unprepared medically for the carnage created by the war, nursing sisters were called upon more and more to take over the duties in hospitals both North and South. Their meticulous care of patients greatly improved the survival rate of the patients and won the hearts of Catholics and Non-Catholics alike. Their attention to detail coupled with their vow of chastity, obedience and poverty[7] caused them to be in great demand by most surgeons. These vows allowed them to work with men in the medical setting without reprisal from Victorian Society.

Their obedience to God forbade them from treating patients of a different color, religion or political view any different from the white catholic patients. They viewed all as children of God and treated them as such. They were discouraged from expressing political views, to participate in political debate or to be known to side with any political or governmental entity. The strict separation of Church and State was

---

[6] Jolly, Ellen Ryan; *"Nuns of the Battlefield"*

[7] Vow of chastity (to never marry or have intercourse with an earthly man), poverty (to not own property of any kind) and Obedience (to do God's bidding in the form of the clergy or Mother Superior).

enforced within the communities. This alone earned them the right from both North and South to cross picket lines freely without any type of hindrance and provided some modicum of protection from many of the officers that knew of their work.

What their vow of poverty meant for the governments that requested their help was that payment was often not required in return for their services. If payment was made, it was to the Mother-house. The nursing sisters also shared rooms and frequently beds, preferring to sleep in rotations so as to ensure a certain number of nurses on duty at any given time and to free beds for those patients in their care.

As the war progressed, the Sisters worked further a field in their efforts to relieve the medical shortage. Sisters from teaching communities worked as nurses. So many Sisters became involved that whole religious communities were reduced to the minimal staff required to continue their work within their lay communities. As the war surged around them, other religious communities also played an important part in nursing as their chapels and vacant schoolrooms were enlisted as short term field hospitals and barracks for severely ill.

A portion of sisters worked in hospital camps that moved every few months to new battlefields needing medical facilities.

The logistical nightmare of moving wounded Northern soldiers from field hospitals in Southern territories to hospitals safe in the North was solved by loading barges with wounded and sending a small number of nursing sisters with them to journey up the Mississippi River northward to safe hospitals. Frequent stops were made in Springfield, MO; Keokuk, IA and Peoria, IL as well as numerous smaller communities. These courageous women could be considered our first naval nurses.

Sisters were occasionally seen working on the battlefields while bullets flew all around them. Though this was rare, one Sister was even reported to have bullet holes through her habit!

While many Catholic solders' spiritual needs went unattended by priests due to the scarcity of priests available to work with the army (approximately 70), the Sisters from 21 religious Communities nursed the sick and injured with a strong dimension of pastoral care. The Sisters were sought after by physicians familiar with their work in hospitals and they represent between 30% and 35% of total nurses working with ill and injured soldiers. They were preferred for their ability to follow orders with discretion and were experience in initiating independent judgment and managing institutions. Lay women represent 5-7% of the nursing staff and the remainder being male. Although historians can never seem to agree on many details, they all agree that the women religious did serve an important medical and social role during the American Civil War helped to open a new frontier for women in the medical field.

(Photo Reference 3)

A Daughter of Charity working as a nurse during war.

Chapter 2

Life as a Nun

Now that an understanding of history has been attained, we must undertake to clarify the role of a Catholic Sister even further. In this chapter we will explain the steps these women followed from candidacy to professed Sister within a Community. Their work and studies will also be briefly reviewed and the basic terminology and assembly of their dress will be explained as well.

The American Civil War Era[8] nestles within an Era popularly called the Victorian Era[9]. This was a time in which England had on its throne a young queen who was found of finery and frippery. Very strict, unwritten, moral rules regarding behavior and manners were followed, especially by the upper class. Young ladies were deemed socially unacceptable if they were touched by a hint that they may have strayed from these rules of the genteel society.

Young ladies were usually accepted as postulants between the ages of fourteen and thirty. The ages varied form one Order to another. A young lady who reached the age of thirty was considered "long in the tooth" when life expectancy was only 60 years of age.

Mother Houses had to be self sufficient if they were to maintain their independence from male guardianship. One of the ways they did this was to require a dowry. While this was held in a trust fund, and managed by a trustee of the community, in the event the Sister left the Order, funds were often invested and the profit or interest used to promote the welfare of the inhabitants. This practice also had the desired effect of ensuring the applicants were of "good moral stock".

Upon the death of the Sister these monies then reverted to the community for use in their work. Almost always, monetary gifts to the Order were also offered with the dowry to ensure their acceptance. On occasion, gifts of land or buildings have also been recorded as being accepted as part of the dowry or gifts to the Order.

Women that proved themselves of good moral character and had a skill needed within the Community would also be accepted without such a dowry. However, this was a rare occasion since most of the lower class felt the need to work in order to support younger siblings or parents that had fallen ill due to poor work and living conditions and poor health care.

---

[8] 1861 - 1865
[9] reigned as queen from 1837 to 1901

Along with a dowry, applicants were given a list of items they were required to bring with them. This was often referred to as a trousseau. Among that list were items of necessity such as under pinnings, linen, sturdy shoes and plain black cape. They were furnished with a black work dress and a thin black veil called a simple veil – visibly different than the black veil of the professed Sisters. These items differentiated them from the lay and staff members.

Mother Houses would take applicants only twice a year and each individual was monitored carefully for compatibility with the goals of the Community[10] during her first eighteen months of working with the community. It is this first year and a half which is the most critical for the Postulate and Novice.

It takes approximately 42 months[11] for a woman to become a fully Professed Sister (one who had taken her final or perpetual vows).

1st 6 months		Entrance into the convent and becomes a postulant. Religious education begins.
6 months	1st retreat	Request acceptance into the community as Novice. This is the Conical year during which the Novice wears a white veil.
12 months	2nd retreat	Religious training continues as well as physical training and work rotations within the infirmary.
18 months	3rd retreat	Temporary professed vows, receive a black veil. Religious education increases and career training begins.
24 months	4th retreat	Career training steps up and nursing education within the convent begins.
30 months	5th retreat	Second set of temporary vows. Enters nursing college.
36 months	6th retreat	No changes in education through this period. Religious contemplation is undertaken with much vigor.
42 months	7th retreat	Final perpetual vows. May enter medical college.

Applicants entered a Novitiate. This was a large building in which they received training in the foundations of their religion throughout their time as Postulants and Novices. On entering, the applicants left behind all

---

[10] Community goals may differ in that one may concentrate on education of the young while another may focus on nursing of the poor.

[11] Information is usually available from individual Motherhouses.

worldly concerns and claim to property. The only possessions they held were the clothes they wore and dowry held in trust for them. The applicants were accepted as postulants only during entrance dates twice a year. This allowed for the equality of training. Postulants were housed in dormitory rooms with ticking mattresses stuffed with straw, a washing stand and a crucifix hanging on the wall. They were also issued one pillow. The Postulants were housed separately from the Novices and the professed nuns. This stark setting would be their refuge for the first six months of convent life.

During this time they were required to follow a strict schedule. Variance to this schedule, as with other infractions of rules, resulted in a penance and prayer for guidance and strength to hold fast to the Communities Rules. Within that schedule, were many hours of meditation and prayer in chapel. Also included were a study of church history, community history, and the foundation of their religion and chores in and around the Novitiate. Training was often strenuous and exacting and chores usually rotated among the Postulants with a Sister of the Order (called a Novice Mistress) overseeing their efforts. If any penance were required due to dereliction of duty or failure of some sort, the Novice Mistress would bestow out the required penance. Penance was not meant as a punishment but as a learning tool and an opportunity to ask for guidance in everyday struggles.

If a certain behavior (such as being late to prayer or class) was repeated many times, this resulted in a visit to Mother Superior. If the behavior could not be corrected and the Postulant required more than one visit, she was deemed unsuited to convent life and sent back to her family.

At the end of the six months, the Postulants would be required to attend a retreat. During Mass on the last day of the retreat, each Postulant would be dressed in a wedding gown. Then, one by one, each would walk down the isle of the chapel and in a special ceremony receive their habit, white veil and their new name. A small lock of hair was symbolically shorn at this time, thusly beginning their Conical year.

The Conical Year

Their first full year of training was even more rigorous than before. In addition to their continued training in religious foundation, they were also required to learn to read and speak in Latin and English. They were also required to do part of the chores necessary to the running of the Novitiate, including handwork, gardening, cleaning, cooking, laundry, sewing, and rotations in the convent infirmary. All of these tasks were rotated throughout the convent so each could learn the duties of each of the professed sisters. Of course, there were the obligatory chapel services several times each day to say the Small Offices and for Mass.

As each novice grew confident within her assignment, she was given more responsibility. Reports of her progress were made to the council and careful watch was kept over each novice's progress and training. During this period the novice is said to be in formation (a period of formation of their religious foundation). If a novice did not do well at the assignment and seemed truly unhappy, reassignment elsewhere was not uncommon.

Retreats were offered twice a year and consisted of a group of Sisters concentrating on spiritual strengthening through prayer, meditation, and a series of talks given by a priest and, most often, complete Silence was maintained with the exception of the speaker. At the end of the retreat during Mass, special ceremonies would be held when a Postulant received her habit, a novice made her temporary vows and professed Sisters would make their second set of temporary vows or permanent ones.

Once the Sisters had become professed, they would move to the Motherhouse and begin training for their professional life. This training was often in the form of apprenticeship with an experienced Sister. They would be housed in stark rooms called cells in which only a bed, a crucifix on the wall, a small dresser and a wardrobe for clothing.

(Illustration reference 4)

Work outside of the Motherhouse may be assigned for purposes of training and for charity work. This was by no means the only training they received. They frequently trained in different areas according to their temperament and interest so they would be flexible within the Motherhouse and prevent potential burnout by having frequent

28

reassignments throughout their entire working life. Remember, once they took permanent vows, the Sisters were there for their entire life.

Professed Sisters

Each Sister would then interview with council members to determine their willingness to continue in their chosen path and their suitability in their assignments. Some Orders allowed permanent vows to be taken at this time while others required a second set of temporary vows. The Sisters of Charity decided on the merits of each Novice, while the Daughters of Charity never made permanent vows. If permanent vows were made, a silver or gold wedding band was worn on the "ring finger" of either the right or the left hand depending on the community they belonged to. Their black veils reveal them as having taken the vows of Chastity, Poverty and Obedience (the obedience being to God's word).

It is during this time that each must decide if they will remain cloistered (if the Order allows choice) or if they will work with the community outside of the Mother House. Training in their chosen profession intensifies. Work is not limited to their profession, however. They continue to share the chores of keeping the Mother House running smoothly and often take on the responsibility of teaching the Novices and Postulants. Everyone is responsible for the fiscal responsibility of the Community. Charity works, after all, cost money. The Community as a whole will work on projects to bring money into the coffers. This might include the selling of access produce from the garden, the raising of dairy cows, milking and making cheese and butter. Hand written bibles became a thing of the past after the printing press was invented, however hand illustrations of the pages continued to be popular into the mid 19th century. Bookbinding and producing publications, painting of miniatures, fine embroidery work, spinning of wool and weaving cloth were all viable occupations for idle hands.

Some Orders also boarded some of their students in dormitories. Their schools were considered elite for women who would eventually attend college. Subjects would range from English, reading and writing, math and social studies to Latin, French, art and religious studies. Young ladies were also taught social graces, sewing and hand arts.

Their classes were not limited to young women. Many young men also attended their schools. Those that completed their education in the Catholic schools would go on to business colleges or medical schools. The Sisters were a dominating influence in education of the young in this country. As reported in the previous chapter, many of these teaching Orders also worked as nurses during the war.

Even before the war, orphanages were a precious commodity in a day and age when medical cures were almost as dangerous as the diseases being treated. Some of the hardships that often separated families permanently were war, famine, Indian hostilities and disease.

Much of this country was considered wild and untamable. It was a daily struggle to stay alive. Many unfortunate accidents resulted in children left without adult care. With the advent of Civil War this became an even greater problem as disease and battle claimed many lives.

Orphanages were often attached to a school. If a Sister did not teach, she cared for the children and kept the orphanage running. Supplies were often very dear and the barter system was widely used to keep food and supplies available. Somehow the Sisters always kept their charges fed, even if they themselves did not eat.

It was also during this time that many of the southern women who joined the order, particularly in New Orleans, brought along their slave women as part of their dower or gifts to the Order. Many a discussion was held between the Mother Superiors of these Communities and the Priests that served as their advisors on the subject of what to do with these women. It was finally decided to allow these black women a choice of being released back into the public as freed, allow them to work within the Mother House as freed women, or to give them the same training they themselves had received and allow them to establish and staff their own convent. Many black women chose to help establish a black community rather than return to a war ravaged community as freed slaves.

In New Orleans, the care the Sisters provided for their charges during war time, so impressed the city fathers of that they included in their city charter that "No Sister of any Order shall be charged for transportation within our city limits. Thus is our debt to the Sisters for their care of our children is discharged." To this day that still holds true!

The Daily Life of a Nun

The following section is paraphrased sections from the book "The Daily Life of a Religious" which talks about how to approach every day tasks as a religious person. To gain the full impact you must read the text in its entirety.

"Do all things well, because all things are done for God." Is the watch word for the Sisters. From the very beginning of their training they are taught that all things they do, no matter how menial, are done for God. How would one dare to offer God anything but perfection? Actions should be cloaked with the highest value and dignity and the utmost sincerity.

The Sisters learn that God claims the consecration of the whole of our thoughts, our affections, and our time. In these things consists our life; and let the first of all these be given to God, that He may sanctify the remainder. "Let every one on awaking," He said, "sigh towards Me from the depths of his heart; and by that sigh let him beg of Me to accept and perfect all his acts during the day; and thus he will draw Me to himself, and I will become the life of his soul, even as his soul is the life of his body." He said another time: "I desire you to open your heart to My heart when you open your eyes to the light and draw your first breath."

Little prayers that are said on putting on each portion of the religious dress are full of the spirit of ancient devotion. The habit of a religious is the livery of Christ, the kiss with which they salute it on first assuming it in the morning, reminds them there is attached an indulgence. This kissing the habit, customary with all religious, was a point of particular devotion with some Saints, notably with Saint John Berchmans, S.J.

Likewise, as God is alpha and omega[12] of their life, He should also be the last thought before we close our eyes at night. Nightly obligations require that we remove our habit with care so as to rise again the next morning with equal care.

And so, it is important to reflect this "God above all" attitude in everything you do. Only then can you emulate the willingness of the Sisters to spend their lives in constant praise and work for God.

Daily offices are a series of devotions and prayers. Why are they called offices? 'The word is taken to signify the principal duty of one's state or condition of life. "A man who holds any office is bound to fulfill the duties pertaining to it before engaging in any others; they take precedence of all else besides and make up the business of his life."[13] So too is it with a Sister. She has many duties, many offices of charity, and many works which give glory to God and are of benefit to mankind. These duties for God are the first business of her life. It follows as a matter of course that her chief care must be to do this duty well.'

Work is a Divine institution. It is perhaps the oldest of all God's institutions. Work is of three kinds and may be divided under the three heads of manual labor, study, and teaching.

The first kind of work is manual labor such as the ordinary household duties in which one must take part as a portion of daily life, as is other active but less laborious occupations.

Bodily labor humbles the flesh and it humbles the spirit and so, it was given as a means of sanctification, as a daily homage of adoration, and as a part of that war upon sensuality and pride, the dual disease of body and soul. In order to do so, labor must be completed with consideration and reflection; love; and the pure and simple desire to please God. Father Le Blanc enumerates the different advantages to be derived from manual labor as follows: 1. The more humiliating or hard the labor is the more it satisfies

---

[12] Alpha and omega are the first and last letters of the Greek alphabet and are used to indicate the first and the last, the beginning and the end.

[13] Raphael, Mother Frances, O.S.D., *The Daily Life of a Religious*

the debt of past sins. 2. It is a remedy against temptations. 3. Work is the mother of courage, generosity of spirit, and other charitable virtues, because it is the enemy of laziness. 4. It has the special privilege of gaining us joy at the hour of death.

The second and third types of labor are teaching and study, and must also be included under the head of labor. Considering how large a portion of our own time is given to occupations of this kind, it is certainly important for us often to meditate how these duties can be well done and made spiritual actions. Intellectual labor in itself is more likely to become unspiritual than manual labor, because it is more absorbing to the mind, engages the thoughts and because it lays the mind open to attacks of vanity and interrupts the silence of the soul. The duty of teaching has to be performed in a particular spirit and surrounded by a rampart of prayer in order to render it safe and profitable to the soul.

The same may be said of every kind of active work of charity. These works must spring from some more supernatural principle than mere compassion and generosity, in order to harmonize with religious life. They must be performed with an intention more divine and spiritual than the love of usefulness.

A religious must, therefore, have something of this love in her heart to enable her to undertake any active work in the religious spirit. As far as possible she must get rid of any notion that she is a hospital-nurse or a schoolmistress; and she must work only because, as the spouse of Jesus, He calls her in His love to minister to Him.

St. Francis of Sales[14] one day made the remark that "I would always," he said, "make more account of little faults than of great ones. Great faults in their own nature inspire horror and it is easier to avoid them. Moreover, fidelity in little things is a test of love." And so, I charge you with minding the little faults with greater care than the larger faults as these are what will give away that you care naught for the work of those Sisters that have gone before us, but, in your own elevation within the Community.

"If we wish to acquire the blessed habit of pleasing God in great things, we must begin by pleasing Him in trifles. In trifles more, perhaps, than in what is great; because trifles do not expose us to the danger of vainglory so much as actions of a more excellent nature; trifles, therefore, are all for God."[15]

---

[14] Raphael, *The Daily Life of a Religious*
[15] Direct quote from: Raphael, *The Daily Life of a Religious*

Basic underpinnings were the same for the Sisters as they were for any lady of the day. In fact most Postulants were required to bring a trousseau with them on arrival. What follows is a list of requirements from one convent.

- Four pair black stockings (either cotton or wool knit)
- One pair garters
- Four pair bloomers
- Two chemises
- Two white nightgowns
- Two modesty slips
- Two petticoats (either black or white)
- Two pair black sturdy boots

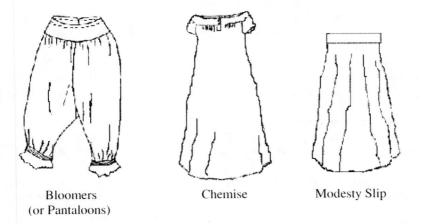

Bloomers   Chemise   Modesty Slip
(or Pantaloons)

Each piece of the trousseau were to be new or in good repair as they had to last for a long time. Usually these under-pinnings were plain—no lace or embroidery were permitted on personal clothing. Corsets were not permitted in the convent as they prevented the flexability to work, contributed to body weakness and to vanity. Sometimes they bound their breasts to minimize feminine curves.

Over the under pinnings came the first piece of clothing to be modified specifically for the Nun's use. This was the chemise. A sleeveless black or white cotton shift that had pockets sewn onto it's surface in strategic areas. These pockets were reached through slits in the habit.

The habit color varied from one Order to the next. They were black, brown, dark blue, medium blue, white, cream or even pink. Some habits were straight cut. Others had a certain number of pleats, each pleat having a meaning or representing Christ's wounds. In Chapter 6 you will see pictures and descriptions of different habits. Usually habits were wool or linen.

When you create your habit or have it made for you, remember that you will be wearing the habit for two days (three if you wear it on Friday). Wool habits may be washed in cold water if need be. Do not attempt to put them in a dryer though. They will need to hang out to dry and may take as many as 2 or 3 days to completely dry. Hang them inside or outdoors in the shade. Sunlight will fade the color. You can use a medium iron to press out wrinkles when necessary. Often wool can be brushed clean with a clothes brush (If you can, use a brush with natural boar's hair bristles), or sticky roller designed to remove pet hair.

The wool that we use today is a light weight dress wool. This breathes well and does not usually overburden the wearer with heat as some of the heavier weight wools will. Another viable option is to use linen when it is available to you. If not, a cotton blend that looks like linen or a great "linen look" fabric is available that drapes well and is hard for the lay public to distinguish from the actual linen fabric.

Linen also breathes well and can be washed in cool or warm water. It also should be hung to dry. Use the linen setting on your iron to press out wrinkles. It is best to check care instructions on the fabric you purchase. Write them down for future reference.

Both wool and linen can be dry cleaned. However, a word to the wise, once you dry clean you should always dry clean. Once you wash, you should always wash. Be consistent with your care of your habit and it will last a long time.

The "whites" in each of the habits presented in this book I have been able to use a heavy cotton fabric with good results. Linen can be used but is not recommended as cotton holds up to the use better than the linen. By "whites" we refer to the guimpe, bandeau and coif. In the Victorian Era, boiled starch was used in vast quantities for these whites. The item was often dipped in this liquid starch numerous times and allowed to dry to shape between, to obtain the desired stiffness required. I did this faithfully, until one weekend reenactment when it rained continuously. Even though it was a light rain, the starch absorbed the damp and ran down into my face allowing the whole head piece to collapse!

After that I began to vary from historical methods a little. For light starches a spray starch and hot iron works well. For those items that must be heavily starched I begin by adding one or two layers of reinforcing fabric. A trick I learned from a Catholic woman whose mother used to care for the Sisters' habits is to soak the items in clear liquid floor wax. Shape them and allow them to dry. This can be done several times until desired stiffness is aquired. The pieces can then be machine washed and dried. A hot steam pressing turns the fabric pliable and removes wrinkles. Shape and allow to cool. If you need to remove the "starch", follow the instructions on the back of the bottle. I recommend doing this at least once a season as it tends to turn yellow after a time.

Veil is almost always linen. The color depends on the Order and what stage the Sister is at in her training. Usually the postulant wears a shortened version in see through black, a Novice wears white and a professed Sister wears black or combination black with a white under veil.

Bandeau is a type of headband or cap, heavily starched to hold the weight of the veil. Always white and usually cotton.

Coif is a type of hood worn to hide the hair and distinguishing characteristics of the Sister. It is the anchor for all the head gear and it is essential that it fit snugly and correctly. It is white and usually cotton. Not starched or very lightly starched..

Guimpe is a type of collar or short cape and is made of the same fabric and color of the habit dress. Most orders also wear a crucifix at the neck line and the cord is adjusted so that it shows just beneath the hem line of the guimpe. The guimpe is lightly starched for work and heavily starched for chapel.

Scapular is not always worn by the Sisters. These straight pieces of fabric in the same material and color as the habit dress serves to cover the feminine curves and reminds the Sister of her many blessings. When worn, great care must be taken to never sit on the back scapular and never step on the front one. The front scapular may be removed to put on a work apron.

Under-sleeves are usually made of a light material such as cotton, muslin or gauze. They are the same color as the habit with elastic at the top and cuff at the wrist.

The Rosary is usually large with 5 or 15 decades. It is worn at the waist on either right or left side (depending on the Community preference). A woolen cord is worn by some orders instead of a leather belt. These usually have three knots or five knots on the ends to represent the vows, wounds of Christ, or some other remembrances.

The dress of the habit varied in color and style according to Order and Community. Please reference in Chapter 6 under the specific Order or Community you wish to portray.

Some orders wore wedding rings, either on left or right hand. Design and color also depended on the Order or Community. Mother Superior would have worn a second ring of office that was either a monogramed ring or one with a semi-precious stone.

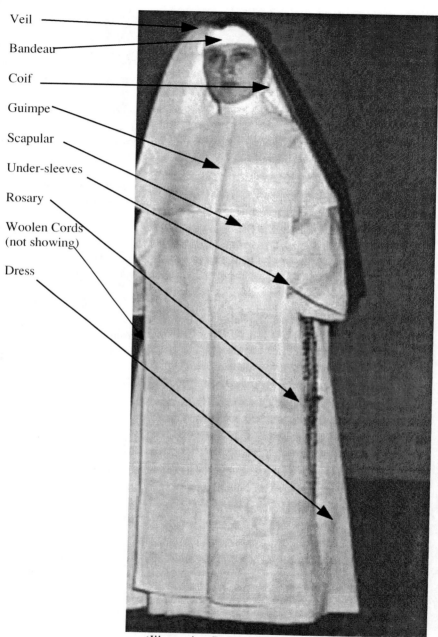

Veil

Bandeau

Coif

Guimpe

Scapular

Under-sleeves

Rosary

Woolen Cords
(not showing)

Dress

(Illustration Reference #14)

The Nun's Command Structure

First let me say that though we work closely with and are attached to medical units, we have a very real and separate command structure that we must adhere to in order to function as Sisters. I will attempt to clear the air here on the command structures and our place within it. The following page will have descriptions and duties. In the Mid-western United States Sisters of St. Brigid is the Mother House Unit and has satellite groups that work within that structure. The following is how we work:

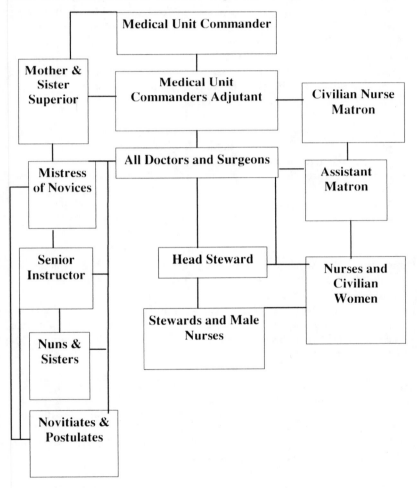

Mother Superior

Description: Head of the Mother House from which all satellite groups stem. Answerable only to God, The Pope, Rev. Father and the Medical Unit Commander and his adjutant.

Duties: Responsible for rules and regulations within the groups under her. Attends Officers call in absence of Unit Commander and adjutant. Approves training and battlefield scenarios, and Convent purchases. She spproves promotions and penances for Sisters directly under her. She leads prayers and directs mass. She oversees all hospital nursing staff in pre-surgical/surgical arena and field hospital. She coordinates duties of Mistress of Novices and Sister Instructors. She oversees camp duties in absence of Nurse Matron and Assistant Nurse matron. She receives reports and assists as needed the Sister Superior of satellite units and reports to the Medical Unit Commander.

Sister Superior

Description: Head of Satellite group to which she is assigned. Answerable only to God, The Pope, Rev. Father, Mother Superior, and the Medical Unit Commander and his adjutant.

Duties: Duties are virtually the same as for Mother superior with the exception that she does not have responsibility for satellite groups. Reports must be sent monthly to update the mother house with all new regulations, new members and about group activities for approval.

Mistress of Novices

Description: Answerable to Mother/Sister Superior and Unit commander. The Mistress of Novices is considered second in command. Her hands are full with the training of Postulates and Novices.

Duties: Oversees Novices and Postulates in duties, training and scenarios. Arranges shopping trips and time off from duties. Responsible for assignment of penances when warranted and coordinates camp duties with nurse matron.

Senior Instructor

Description: Answers to Mother/Sister Superior, Unit commander, all doctors and surgeons and Mistress of Novices. The Senior Instructor is responsible for the education of the Convent.

Duties: Coordinates and teaches all medical training for all Sisters but, especially for Novices and Postulates.

Sisters/Nuns, Novitiates (white veil) , Postulates (see through veil).

Description: All are considered equal in that none have sway over the other but only Nuns/Sisters may help instruct. Answerable to

Stewards, Surgeons, Senior Instructor, Mistress of Novices, Mother/Sister Superior

Duties: Attend surgical/medical classes and other duties as assigned.

Nurse Matron and Assistant Matron

Description: Head of women nurses and Civilian women. Answerable to Unit commander and commander's adjutant.She works closely with the Mother Superior and Mistress of Novices.

Duties: Approves camp scenarios, purchases for camp, coordinates camp and post-surgical duties with Mistress of Novices or Mother Superior, oversees civilian staff and any Sisters placed under her for the purpose of helping with camp duties, may assign women nurses to Mother Superior or Mistress of Novices for hospital duties, When first three in Sister's structure are not available will oversee pre-surgical/surgical/hospital duties as well as her own.

Women Nurses

Description: These women are answerable to all medical staff. May be assigned to surgical/hospital areas under the direction of the Sisters in pre-op or sugrgical areas, or a head matron in post-op areas.

Duties: Duties as assigned.

Civilian women

Description: any women who are not specifically nurses with the unit. This may include women from other units or independent nurses.

Duties: as assigned by Nurse Matron or Assistant Nurse matron.

Illustration reference #5   Rev. Father Hunt

Chapter 3

Choosing an Order

The choice of an Order can be a hard one for someone who is not sure what aspect they would like to emulate. There are many different Orders to choose from. This chapter will give you a knowledge base of the nursing Orders, their habits and some useful information to help you assimilate yourself into the reenacting community as a viable contributor.

The more comfortable you are with your role the better your portrayal will look to the public. Research each of the Orders that interest you. What were the primary functions of the Order? What talent would they have recruited to keep themselves independent? Then, look at your own talents. What do you enjoy doing? How can those talents be incorporated into your portrayal? Later in this chapter we will discuss each of the orders individually in more detail.

The last think to look at is the habit styles of the Orders you are contemplating. Is it a style you would feel comfortable wearing? Keep in mind that you may be making this habit yourself. Habits are currently being custom made. Addresses, e-mail and web site will appear at the end of the book in the information section.

Next, you must decide where you are going to wear the habit. Will you be in camp, on a battlefield or at a presentation? Keep this in mind as you look at habit styles. A sprawling, wing like cap would be too cumbersome (and downright dangerous) for a battlefield nurse, but fine for a hospital nurse and great for presentations.

Now let's put this in action and see how it works: Jane has a talent for hand work and organizing. Her research shows her that there were nine Orders that taught the female children of well to do families (which would have included hand work). Five Orders in Northern States and four in Southern States.

Although, this is Jane's primary talent, portraying a teaching Nun from one of these Orders would mean that she would stay in the encampment for the most part. Though, she could go watch the battle in progress. Leslie thinks that would be great. She has no interest in going out on the battlefield. However, Jane really wants to be "out there" where the action is.

Her other talent of organization may do just that. Several of the Orders that concentrated on nursing also required administrative staff to help organize the hospital. Of those Orders, Jane chooses a Southern based Order whose habit style would not hinder her on the battlefield as she organizes the field hospital and triages the wounded on their arrival. As Jane learns more about nursing, the more real her portrayal will seem.

Leslie on the other hand can take over the role of teaching at the camp. While Jane organizes the hospital, the girls gathered around Leslie to learn how to spin, tat, sew a straight line or obtain nursing instruction. Each of the girls fit talent and personality to their roles as a nun.

Battlefield Etiquette

If you are part of a medical unit already, or have been working as a nurse with one, more power to you. You probably already know most of what I'm going to tell you. But, don't skip this part. We all can use reminders and there may be some new tips you don't know. If you haven't yet been on the battlefield, there are some things you should know before hand.

Always present yourself to the officers of the medical unit several hours before the start of battle. Do so in the dress you plan to wear on the field so the officers know what you look like and what problems or opportunities you may present for them. This gives them time to verse you in their protocol and give you your assignment. It is even better when you can spend the whole day with them and get well acquainted with the way they do things. Offer to help with camp duties! That always makes people welcome you into the ranks quicker. Attend meetings for nurses and listen well. Don't be disappointed if they request you change into a different dress or decline to take you with them. They may be filled up with nurses or require that you wear a certain type of dress or uniform (or they may require you to be a nun).

Never, ever attempt to go on the battlefield as an independent. It is far too, dangerous and you will be removed from the field. Follow the rules of the unit you are working with and always obey orders immediately.

Get to know who you are working with. Know the real life medical people and what the signal is for a real emergency. Know how to get help when you need it.

Never, walk in front of a canon or live rifle fire. Beside heat stroke, this is the cause of most accidents on the field. Those soldiers on the field are safety conscious and will hold up the battle until you move on your own or are removed from the field.

Drink plenty of fluids before battle time. Keep your canteen filled with fresh water. Inform the persons in charge of the medical unit of any medications you are taking or any medical problems you have.

Wool habits may be the proper thing to wear, but, if you are prone to heat strokes or take medication that makes you easily succumb to heat then by all means have your habit made of linen instead. Linen is lighter than wool and is entirely appropriate. Minimize your underclothes on those days of 102° weather. Make them of very light weight material and loose fitting. This will help move air through the garments and evaporate skin moisture, keeping the wearer cooler.

Most of all enjoy what you are doing and do it safely. Don't skip meals and drink plenty of fluids. If you are not a permanent part of a medical unit, present yourself to the medical unit of your choice several hours before battle time. If the unit you are working with sends it's nurses out onto the field, be aware at all times of what is going on around you. Listen to instructions and obey them immediately.

Scenarios are skits that act out how something might have happened. An example of this is a scenario portraying sick call. Here you would round up soldiers to attend a sick call and have a doctor prescribe medications (sugar pills and innocuous liquids) and treatments the nurses will then prepare and administer. These scenarios draw in visitors and serve as a teaching tool. They are often impressive but everyone must be aware of what is happening and be doing things safely.

The Nursing Orders

1. Daughters of Charity of St. Vincent de Paul
    -Emmetsburg, Maryland   44
2. Sisters of Mercy -Pittsburgh, Pennsylvania   49, 50
3. Sisters of Mercy -Cincinnati, Ohio   49, 51
4. Sisters of Mercy -Vicksburg, Mississippi   49, 51
5. Sisters of Mercy -Chicago, Illinois   49, 52
6. Sisters of Mercy -Baltimore, Maryland   49, 52
7. Sisters of Mercy -New York, New York   49, 53
8. Sisters of the Holy Cross—Notre Dame   54
9. Sisters of Charity - of Cincinnati   57
10. Sisters of Charity - of New York   59
11. Sisters of Charity - of Nazareth   60
12. Sisters of the Poor of St. Francis –Cincinnati, Ohio   62
13. Sisters of Saint Dominic -Springfield, Kentucky   63
14. Sisters of Saint Dominic -Memphis Tennessee   65
15. Sisters of St. Joseph - Wheeling, West Virginia   67
16. Sisters of St Joseph – Philadelphia, Pennsylvania   68
17. Sisters of Charity of Our Lady of Mercy
    - Charleston, S.C.   69
18. Sisters of Providence - St. Mary of the Woods,
    Indiana   71
19. Sisters of Our Lady of Mount Carmel
    - New Orleans   72
20. Sister of St. Ursula - Galveston, TX.   74
    Sisters of St. Brigid—Kingsport, Missouri   76

The garb of the Daughters of Charity is still that of the peasant girl of 1633. Once was inconspicuous on the streets of Paris, the white cornette and blue gown of the Daughter of Charity is easily identified, even in a convention hall crowded with a thousand nuns of various Orders. She also wears a guimpe that is squared in front and black belt with black rosary to the left side.

St Vincent de Paul gathered a group of pious country girls, trained them under St. Louise de Marillac and sent them out to the garrets of Paris. In a short time they were in demand everywhere. In 1809, Elizabeth Ann Seaton established a branch of these Sisters at Emmitsburg, Maryland. The needs of the poor determine the works of the Daughters of Charity. After her name she signs these letters: "u. d. o. c. s. o. t. s. p. ". They mean: "Unworthy Daughter of Charity, servant of the sick poor".

The Daughters of Charity, since their beginnings have followed in the wake of wars. The Emmitsburg Sisters are documented to have been at Gettysburg on July 4-9, 1863, as well as Harper's Ferry and Bolivar Heights, Richmond, VA Hospital, Winchester, VA; Frederick City, MD; and Washington D.C. Hospitals. Their work have made then renown in the United States and indeed around the world.

Within a few days after the official declaration of the Civil War, these Sisters were in charge of two large military hospitals in Richmond. Other hospitals were quickly established in the war zone, and were filled with the sick and wounded almost before the hospitals were completed and ready for their care.

Incomplete Civil War records note that at least two hundred and thirty-two Sisters were among those from Emmitsburg caring for both Northern and Southern armies. They responded quickly and many names of those that entered service were not recorded. It is probable that many more than that responded to the need for nurses. Two hundred and twenty Sisters served with the ambulance crews. They also served on hospital ships and transports, in the tent, field and permanent hospitals, in the isolated camps reserved for contagious cases, and in the military prisons. These Sisters were particularly successful in the treatment of the insane because of the special training they received. The Sisters were often found on the firing line of many battlefields, placing themselves in the same danger as the soldiers they cared for. When news of arriving Sisters spread through the towns crowds of citizens welcomed them. Cheers went up in camp hospitals on the site of arriving Sisters.

The Sisters not only went to the war, but the war also came to them. One or the other forces while passing through several times occupied their little valley in Emmitsburg. During the occupation for hours or days, they helped to feed starving men with fresh baked breads and soups or stews made from dwindling supplies. The Sisters often went hungry so that the men could have a meal.

The following is a list of known Daughters of Charity that served as nurses on the battlefield and in the hospitals in the town of Gettysburg.

Mother Mary Ann Simeon Norris

Sr. Mary Gertrude Balfe
Sr. Mary Petroniklla Breen
Sr. Mary Catherine Chrismer
Sr. Mary Matilda Coskery
Sr. Mary Genevieve Dodthage
Sr. Mary Adele Durm
Sr. Mary Farrell
Sr. Mary Anastasia Felix
Sr. Mary Aloysia Daley
Sr. Mary Serena Klemkiewiez
Sr. Mary Loretta Mullery
Sr. Mary Joseph Murphy
Sr. Mary Victorine Petry

Sr. Mary Gabriella Rigney
Sr. Mary David Slamon
Sr. Mary Ameliana Schroeder
Sr. Mary Elizabeth Schroeder
Sr. Mary Anselm Shaw
Sr. Mary Raphael Smith
Sr. Mary Oswald Spalding
Sr. Mary Ann Steckel
Sr. Mary Angela Walsh
Sr. Mary Genevieve McDonough
Sr. Mary Annie McShane
Sr. Mary Camilla O'Keefe

The following Sisters formed a part of the ambulance Corps who served on land and on water in the South and in the North. These names will shine forever in the history of the Catholic Church:

Sr. Mary Phillip Barry
Sr. Mary Euphenia Blenkisop
Sr. Mary Martha Bridgman
Sr. Mary Amie Butterly
Sr. Mary Laura Carroll
Sr. Mary Marie Louise Caulfield
Sr. Mary Matilda Comstock
Sr. Mary Mary Cummiskey
Sr. Mary Agatha Devlin
Sr. Mary Baptista Dowds
Sr. Mary Catharine Driscoll

Sr. Mary Donata Bell
Sr. Mary Susanna Brandel
Sr. Mary Thomas Bridgman
Sr. Mary Margaret Carr
Sr. Mary Henrietta Casey
Sr. Mary Juliana Chatard
Sr. Mary Consolata Conlon
Sr. Mary Felicita D'Aunoy
Sr. Mary John Douglass
Sr. Mary Vincent Doyle
Sr. Mary Vincent Flemming

Sr. Mary Marianna Flynn
Sr. Mary Dorothia Hanigan
Sr. Mary Terea Healy
Sr. Mary Aloysius Daley
Sr. Mary Aloysia Kane
Sr. Mary Mary Anges Kelly
Sr. Mary Valentine Latourandais
Sr. Mary Ellen Leddy
Sr. Mary Remi Lee
Sr. Mary Louise Le Gros
Sr. Mary Frances Meakin
Sr. Mary Rose Mullin
Sr. Mary Geraldine Murphy
Sr. Mary Ambrosia McDevitt
Sr. Mary Beata McFaul
Sr. Mary Thomas McSwiggin
Sr. Mary Madeline O'Brien
Sr. Mary Georgia O'Connor
Sr. Mary Eustolia O'Donnell
Sr. Mary Florence O'Hare
Sr. Mary Mary O'Neil
Sr. Mary Leontine Poirer
Sr. Mary Urbana Pole
Sr. Mary Emerito Wuinlan
Sr. Mary Rosina Quinn
Sr. Mary Simeon Wuinn
Sr. Mary Alexia Raynice
Sr. Mary Catharine Rectanwald
Sr. Mary Aloysia Reed
Sr. Mary Ellen Relihan
Sr. Mary Satanislaus Roche
Sr. Mary Mary Romer

Sr. Mary Walburga Gehring
Sr. Mary Rosalie Harrington
Sr. Mary Angela Heath
Sr. Mary Angelica Halloran
Sr. Mary Frances Karrer
Sr. Mary Maria Landry
Sr. Mary Michaella Laurent
Sr. Mary Vincentia Leddy
Sr. Mary Teresa Maxent
Sr. Mary Mary Thomas Maynes
Sr. Mary Ambrosia Morrisette
Sr. Mary Aloysia Morgan
Sr. Mary Mary Ann McAteer
Sr. Mary Clotilde McIlhenny
Sr. Mary Clotilda McSweeny
Sr. Mary Tose Noylan
Sr. Mary Ann Lousie O'Connell
Sr. Mary Blanche Rooney
Sr. Mary Elizabeth Rooney
Sr. Mary Marcelline Salamon
Sr. Mary Philomena Scholl
Sr. Mary Vincent Shea
Sr. Mary Elizabeth Sheil
Sr. Mary Agnes Slavin
Sr. Mary Francis Smith
Sr. Mary Regina Smith
Sr. Mary Josephine Swope
Sr. Mary Appolonia Tiernan
Sr. Mary Clara Trigant
Sr. Mary Joanna Turley
Sr. Mary Cathrine Ulrich

The following Daughters of Charity served at Lincoln Hospital in Washington, D.C.:

Sr. Mary Helen Ryan, Superior

Sr. Mary Rosalie Bouligney
Sr. Mary Annie Gately
Sr. Mary Petrolinna Breen
Sr. Mary Martha Grant
Sr. Mary Loretta O'Connell
Sr. Mary Alphonsus Groell
Sr. Mary Marie Cosgrove
Sr. Mary Sienna Harty
Sr. Mary Ammia Dougherty

Sr. Mary Maria Kenny
Sr. Mary Joseph Dougherty
Sr. Mary Alphonso Lortzman
Sr. Mary Amelia Duffy
Sr. Mary Stanislaus Mahoney
Sr. MaryGenevieve Emers
Sr. Mary Fidelis Manning
Sr. Mary Henrietta Forestall
Sr. Mary Clara Maloney

Sr. Mary Elizabeth Frass
Sr. Mary Francis Mullin
Sr. Mary Aloysia Freckert
Sr. Mary Loretta Mullery
Sr. Mary Genevieve Garvey

Sr. Mary Urban McNeill
Sr. Mary Luciana Oliver
Sr. Mary Cotilda O'Neill
Sr. Mary Leontine Pfaff
Sr. Mary Mary Ellen Reardon

The following Sisters nursed the soldiers in Satterlee Hospital, Philadelphia, Pennsylvania:

Sr. Mary Gonzaga Grace, Superior

Sr. Mary Clestine Adelsburga
Sr. Mary Adeline Byrne
Sr. Maria Boniface
Sr. Mary Rosalie Bouligney
Sr. Mary Petronilla Breen
Sr. Mary Genevieve Cavanaugh
Sr. Mary Louise Collins
Sr. Mary Philippa Connolly
Sr. Mary De Chantal Costello
Sr. Mary Mray Cremen
Sr. Mary Joseph Cummin
Sr. Mary Aloysia Daley
Sr. Mary Amelia Davis
Sr. Mary Elizabeth Freze
Sr. Mary Josephine Gamel
Sr. Mary Genevieve Garvey
Sr. Mary Francis Griffin
Sr. Mary Cecilia Groell
Sr. Mary Magdalen Groell
Sr. MaryMartha Lynch
Sr. Mary Neri Mathews
Sr. Mary Bernard Moore
Sr. Mary Stella Moran
Sr. Mary Euphrasia Mattingly
Sr. Mary Gabriella McCarthy
Sr. Mary Clementine McCaffrey
Sr. Mary Francis McDonald
Sr. Mary Loretta McGee
Sr. Mary Teresa McKenna
Sr. Mary Catharine McQuaid
Sr. Mary Maria Noonan
Sr. Mary Deonysia O'Keefe
Sr. Mary Sylveria O'Neill
Sr. Mary Angeline Reilly
Sr. Mary Severina Relihan

Sr. Mary Alice Delahunty
Sr. Mary Amie Dougherty
Sr. Mary Ann Joseph Dougherty
Sr. Mary Eliza Cougherty
Sr. Mary Jane Doglas
Sr. MaryJosephine Edelin
Sr. Mary Bernard Farrell
Sr. Mary Bernardine Farrell
Sr. Mary Marcella Finnigan
Sr. Mary Julia Fitzgerald
Sr. Mary Generosa Foley
Sr. Mary Vincent Foster
Sr. Mary Cecilia Harty
Sr. Mary Margaret Hepp
Sr. Mary Mary Harmer
Sr. Mary Laurentia Kane
Sr. Mary Josephine Kelleher
Sr. Mary Gabriel Kraft
Sr. Mary Eloise laCroix
Sr. Mary Angela Mahoney
Sr. Mary Alex Merceret
Sr. Mary Martha Moran
Sr. Mary Marie Mulkern
Sr. Mary Alponsa McBride
Sr. Mary Irene McCourt
Sr. Mary Agnes McDermott
Sr. Mary Cornelia McDonnell
Sr. Mary Clare McGerard
Sr. Mary Alphonsa McNichols
Sr. Mary Felix McQuaid
Sr. Mary Anastasia O'Donnell
Sr. Mary Annie O'Leary
Sr. Mary Felicita Puls
Sr. Mary Ann Teresa Roche
Sr. Mary Onsesime Rosenthal

47

Sr. Mary Dolores Smith
Sr. Mary Joseph Sinnott
Sr. Mary Julia Sheehan
Sr. Mary Eleanor Tyler
Sr. MaryAugustine Valentine
Sr. Mary Vincenta Waltzing
Sr. Mary Clotilda Welty
Sr. Mary Euphrasia Wittenanes

Sr. Mary Vincent Saudners
Sr. Mary Ann Mary Shaughnessy
Sr. Mary Marina Tragesser
Sr. Mary Pacifica Ulrich
Sr. Mary Xavier Van Drome
Sr. Mary Agnes Weaver
Sr. Mary Henrietta Wise
Sr. Mary Delphine Wivelle

The Sisters of Mercy habit is black wool, plaited at the waist; a cincture of black leather, a white guimpe with large white collar, a black veil, rosary, and a silver ring.

"Seven Sisters of Mercy were the gracious gift of Ireland to this great nation...", writes the author of Nuns of the Battlefield. On December 21st, 1843 the first Convent of Mercy was established in the United States. Catherine Elizabeth McAuley founded the Order of Mercy in Ireland on the banks of the Liffey in 1831. On January 24, 1834, Francis Warde was the first novice professed in the chapel of the Mother House on Baggot Street. She was destined to become the foundress of the Order of Mercy in the United States.

When the invitation to come to the United States (known as the foreign mission) was extended to the Carlow Community Mother Xavier was blessed with her fondest wish to be the first of her institute to touch the soil where her country-people were immigrating. Six Religious accompanied Mother Xavier across the Atlantic and the Alleghenies. They included *Sister Mary Josephine Cullen, who was niece to His Eminence Paul Cardinal Cullen, Archbishop of Dublin, Sisters Mary Aloysia and Mary Elizabeth Strange, sisters by blood whose uncle was His Eminence Nicholas Cardinal Wiseman, first Archbishop of Westminster, Sister Veronica McDarby "the joy of the Community," Sister Philomena Reid "a novice of great promise," and Miss Margaret O'Brien, a postulant of distinguished lineage, and later known in religion as the Rev. Mother Mary Agatha O'Brien, the foundress of the Chicago Community.*

On November 26, 1862 a corps of Sisters from Mercy Hospital, in Pittsburgh took charge of long rows of frame buildings in Washington, D. C. they began their work by caring for one hundred and thirty soldiers just from the front.

By December 8, Washington had become one vast hospital because of it's centralized location. *Terrific battles were fought around the city and almost hourly the rude ambulances delivered at Stanton their bleeding burdens brought in from neighboring battlefields and prisons. Day and often during the entire desolate night, the Sisters were on duty, never failing to render the soldiers ready and sympathetic treatment.*

These Nuns had served long and exacting hours in their own Mercy Hospital in preparation for this new duty. Many of the most distinguished physicians and surgeons of the period staffed this hospital under whose instruction the Sisters had fourteen years in which to become fully equipped for the strenuous hospital duty in "the Stanton" in Washington, D.C. and the West Pennsylvania Military Hospital in the city of Pittsburgh.

It has been said the military physicians and surgeons in Stanton regarded the Sisters as valuable assistants, and oftentimes the nuns had the entire charge of the patients, administering medicines and arranging bandages with deft and skillful hands. [1] Indeed hardships such as lack of nourishment and exposure to the elements as well as diseases and prolonged hours caring for their charges without regard to their own need caused some of these women to pay with their lives for their heroic devotion. Often when rations were limited, as if by a miracle, they secured nourishment for men weakened in the swamps, and the loss of blood from gaping wounds. Worn and weary through sleepless nights they labored on.

A tribute to the Sisters of Mercy by Henry Wadsworth Longfellow:
Other hope had she none, nor wish in life, but to follow
Meekly, with reverent steps, the sacred feet of her Savior,
And with light in her looks, she entered the chamber of sickness,
Moistening the feverish lip, and the aching brow, and in silence
Closing the sightless eyes of the dead, and concealing their faces,
Where on their pallets they lay, like drifts of snow on the road-side.
Many a languid head, upraised as the Sister entered,
Turned on its pillow of pain to gaze while she passed, for her presence
Fell on their hearts like a ray of sun on the walls of a prison.

All of the Sisters of Mercy wore the same basic habit. Rosary type may change from one community to another, but not the habit. For all of the Sisters of Mercy the previous description and picture holds true. What follows is the list of names of those Sisters known to have contributed to the Nursing staff of many hospitals and field hospitals. There is no distinction of where they have worked

Sisters of Mercy—Pittsburgh, Pennsylvania

These Sisters worked their miricles in the Statton Hospital and the West Pennsyvania Hospital as well as in "The Field of Tents" (A large field hospital set up on the hill-sides out side of Pittsburg.

Mother Mary Rose Hostetter

Sr. Mary Neri Bowen	Sr. Mary Flavia Byrne
Sr. Mary Regina Cosgrave	Sr. Mary Vincent Delaney
Sr. Mary Helen Devlin	Sr. Mary Borgia Doherty
Sr. Mary Benedict Duffy	Sr. Mary Leo Driscoll
Sr. Mary Odelia Dusch	Sr. Mary Isidore Fisher
Sr. Mary Sebastian Gillespie	Sr. Mary Berchmans Hostetter

Sr. Mary Nolasco Kratzer	Sr. Mary Appolonia Leahy
Sr. Mary Bernard Maher	Sr. Mary Basil McGinn
Sr. Mary Remigius McQuade	Sr. Mary Gonzaga Myers
Sr. Mary Madeleine O'Donnel	Sr. Mary Celestine Rafferty
Sr. Mary de Pazzi Russell	Sr. Mary Augustine Schuck
Sr. Mary de Ricci Tierney	Sr. Mary Stephana Ward

Sisters of Mercy—Cincinnati, Ohio

These Sisters having already won the hearts of Florence Nightengale and Queen Victoria, as well as the people of Turkey andRussia for their unswerving dedication to their patients' care at the Military Hospitals there during the Crimean War, went on to win the hearts of American soldiers.

They first had turned their Third Street Convent into an auxillary hospital and took both Federal and Confederate soldiers into their care. They also served on the battlefield Shilo and broght many wounded back to Cincinnati Hospitals on the specially constructed Hospital Boat, the "*Superior*".[16] It is said that while scores of Sisters of Mercy of the Cincinnati Community did heroic war service only the following eleven names were recorded on the nation's war files

Mother Mary Teresa Maher

Sr. Mary Xavier Cosgrove	Sr. Mary Madeline Curtin
Sr. Mary Teresa Doughtery	Sr. Mary de Sales Douglas
Sr. Mary Joseph Dowling	Sr. Mary Baptist Kane
Sr. Mary Philomena Kenny	Sr. Mary Stanislaus Murphy
Sr. Mary Francis Nunan	Sr. Mary Gertrude O'Dwyer

Sisters of Mercy— Vicksburg, Mississippi

On the 1st through the 4th of July, 1863, Generals Grant and Johnston met at Vicksburg while Generals Robert E. Lee and George G. Meade classed at Gettysburg. The Sisters of Mercy were under shot and shell of the two armies andgve an additional brilliancy to the name of their foundress, Mother Mary Catherine McAuley. The Sisters of Mercy, of Vicksburg were "Nuns of the Battlefield" in the broadest sense. Their unflinching and impartial service to soldiers of both armies as well as the beleaugered people of the city

Mother Mary de Sales Browne

Sr. Mary Vincent Browne	Sr. Mary Philomena Farmer
Sr. Mary Agnes Madigan	Sr. MaryTeresa Newman
Sr. Mary Xavier Poursine	Sr. Mary Agnatia Sumner

---

[16] Jolly, Ellen Ryan; "*The Nuns of the Battlefield*".

Sr. Mary Stehana Warde

Sisters of Mercy— Chicago, Illinois

During the period between 1861 to 1865, Mother Mary Frances Monholland and her commrades of Mercy Hospital gave service in camp hospitals, field hospitals, floating hospitals (one of which was the *Empress*), prisons and quaritined pest-hospitals of the Civil War.

Mother Mary Frances Monholland

Sr. Mary Louise Berry	Sr. Mary Alphonsus Butler
Sr. Mary Raymond Garrity	Sr. Mary Titiana Harkins
Sr. Mary Borromeo Johnson	Sr. Mary Anastasia Lyster
Sr. Mary Elzear McGratton.	Sr. Mary Patricia Reardon
Sr. Mary Bertrand Walsh.	

Sisters of Mercy—Baltimore, Maryland

These Sisters worked in Washington, D. C. at "The Infirmary", "The Old Armory", and thr "Douglas Hospital. It was these Sisters that visited President Lincoln and explained the plight of their patients and lack of provisons. It was to them he presented the written historical message:

"To Whom It May Concern:
On application of the Sisters of Mercy in charge of the Military Hospital in Washington furnish such provisions as they desire to purchase, and charge same to the War Department.
(Signed) Abraham Lincoln" [17]

With these orders in hand the Sisters did indeed make a enormous difference in the outcome of many of the patients in their care.

Mother Mary Collette O'Connor

Sr. Mary Catherine Brown	Sr. Mary Regina Brown
Sr. Mary Veronica Doyle	Sr. Mary Lucy Duffy
Sr. Mary Martha Fitzgerald	Sr. Mary Agatha Flynn
Sr. Mary Veronica Flaherty	Sr. Mary Gertrude Wynne
Sr. Mary Bernard O'Kane	Sr. Mary Anastasia Quinn.
Sr. Mary Ann Rigney	Sr. Mary Patricia Smythe.
Sr. Mary Gonzaga Muihare	Sr. Mary Agnes Moran.
Sr. Mary Stanislaus Mathews	Sr. Mary Cephas Flynn
Sr. Mary Magdalen Healy	Sr. Mary Bernadine Keefer
Sr. Mary Timothy Leddy	

---

[17] Jolly, Ellan Ryan; *"Nuns of the Battlefield"*

Sisters of Mercy—New York, New York

These Sisters worked in the southeastern portion of the North for the most part. They brought supplies, order and cleanliness to the Hammond Military Hospital in Beaufort, North Carolina. Following that they worked at Newberne in what was previously the Governors mansion. When they left for New-York in April of 1863 they invited four of their Negro women to return with them.

Mother Mary Augustine MacKenna

Sr. Mary Elizabeth Callanan	Sr. Mary Martha Corrigan
Sr. Mary Veronica Dimond	Sr. Mary Ignatius Grant
Sr. Mary Paula Harris	Sr. Mary Gertrude Ledwith
Sr. Mary Paul Lennon	Sr. Mary Francis Murray
Sr. Mary Agatha McCarthy	

Mother Mary Madeleine Tobin

Sr. Mary Gerard Ryan	Sr. Mary Aiphonsus Smythe
Sr. Mary Vincent Sweetman	

HISTORY: The Sisters of the Holy Cross were founded at Le Mans, France, in 1841, by the Very Rev. Basil Anthony Moreau. In 11843, four Sisters of the infant Community left France for America and established the first foundation in the New World, at Notre Dame. From its present Motherhouse there, at St. Mary's Convent, the Community has grown. To-day its houses reach from Michigan to Texas and from Massachusetts to California. Institutions under its direction number three liberal colleges, twelve hospitals and infirmaries, four orphanages, and some hundred elementary and secondary schools. Moreover, East Pakistan, Indian, and Sao Paulo, Brazil, witness the foreign mission apostolate of its members; while missions for the Negro and for the neglected Mexicans of the South are conducted in the United States.

PURPOSE: The primary aim of the Sisters of the Holy Cross is personal sanctification; their secondary purpose is the salvation of souls achieved through their apostolate. Their title designates their spirit. To dwell with Our Lady of Sorrows at the foot of the cross in contemplative love and in joyful imitation of the Crucified is the challenge to sanctify presented by their Rule.

QUALIFICATIONS: Young women are admitted to the postulate at the completion of their high school course who: desire to dedicate themselves to the apostolate of Christian education---or nursing---or the foreign missions.

Those desiring to dedicate themselves to the hidden apostolate may be admitted without this requirement.

HABIT: The black habit of the Sisters is characterized by the Rosary of the Seven Dolors worn at their right side, while a blue cord in honor of Mary is worn at the left. A silver heart bearing the image of Our Lady of Sorrows, the patroness and model of the Sisters, is suspended from their circular collar. The head dress is a fluted cap evolved from that of French peasants of the province where the community was founded.

In autumn of 1861 the Govenor of Indiana, Oliver Perry Morton at the request of General Lew Wallace, officially requested twelve Sisters to attend the sick, wounded and dying at the hospital in Cairo, Illinois. These were the first six to respond there.

Mother Angela (Eliza Maria Gillespie)

Sr. Adele (Cathrine Morgan)   Sister Anna (Mary Dorsey)
Sr. Magdalene (Ellen Kiernan)   Sister Veronica (Regina Scholl)
Sr. Winnefred (Catherine McGinn)

On October 21, 1861, the day after the battle of Ball's Bluff, the Very Reverand Edward Sorin, C.S.C. also requested twelve Sisters to attend The sick, wounded and dying in Paducah, Kentucky. Shortly thereafter, another Corps of Sisters was requested for Louisville, Kentucky at the Government Millitary Hospital.

In November yet another group of Sisters departed for Mound City, Illinois to open yet another Military Hospital. In 1862 the area surrounding Mound City was Surrounded with water during the great Ohio River flooding, cutting it off from outside communication. The hospital was evacuated to Jefferson Barracks in St. Louis.

Other places the Sisters worked were Saint Aloysius Hospital on the Potomac River; "The Naval Hospital" in Memphis Tennessee; and the pest-houses in Franklin, Missouri where many of the soldiers so infected were taken. There assisted by the Sanitary Commission they cared for soldiers of both great armies. It was from the Memphis, Mound City and Ciaro groups that corps of Sisters were recruited for government transports which sailed up and down the Mississippi River carrying the sick and wounded from the battlefields to the Sisters' hospitals. The "Red Rover" was one of those floating hospitals and Vicksburg was its destination during the siege. Here the Sisters endured the hardships of the battle along with the soldiers in order to carry their patients out of the distressed city to safety.

Mother Mary Angela Gillespie.	Mother Mary Augustine Anderson
Sr. Mary Gregory Barry	Sr. Mary Angeline Blake
Sr. Mary Rita Brennan	Sr. Mary Ferdinand Bruggerman
Sr. Mary Paula Casey	Sr. Mary Celestine Cavanaugh
Sr. Mary Lydia Clifford	Sr. Mary Isidore Conlin
Sr. Mary Passion Cowley	Sr. Mary Providence Daget
Sr. Mary Bartholomew Darnell	Sr. Mary Anna Dorsey
Sr. Mary Mount Cannel Dougherty	Sr. Mary Helen Fitzpatrick
Sr. Mary Augustine Flanagan	Sr. Mary Alice Flannery
Sr. Mary Aloysius Garen	Sr. Mary Compassion Gleason
Sr. Mary Matilda Hartnet	Sr. Mary Odelia Higgins
Sr. Mary Theodore Kearns	Sr. Mary Felix Kelly
Sr. Mary Irene Keough	Sr. Mary Magdalen Kiernan
Sr. Mary Catherine Kilkenny	Sr. Mary Barbara
Sr. Mary Fidelis Lawler	Sr. Mary Aurelius

Sr. Mary Felicita Mulloy

Sr. Mary Francis Malloy

Sr. Mary Anthony Mannix

Sr. Mary Adele Moran

Sr. Mary Angela Muldoon

Sr. Mary Faustina Morrissey

Sr. Mary Edward Murphy

Sr. Mary Theodosia McCushing

Sr. Mary Rose McDermott

Sr. Mary Winifred McGinn

Sr. Mary Patrick MeQockin

Sr. Mary Eusebia McIntosh

Sr. Mary Conception McIntyre

Sr. Mary Henrietta McLaughlin

Sr. Mary John of the Cross McLaughlin

Sr. Mary Agnes Neville

Sr. Mary Elise O'Brien

Sr. Mary Angelica O'Brien

Sr. Mary Victoria O'Keefe

Sr. Mary Athanasius O'Neill

Sr. Mary de Sales O'Neill

Sr. Mary Bernard Pecord

Sr. Mary Celeste Pomta

Sr. Mary Martha

Sr. Mary Josephine Reilly

Sr. Mary Veronica Scholl

Sr. Mary Bernard Shandley

Sr. Mary Flavia Smith

Sr. Mary Macrina Snow

Sr. Mary Christine Sophia

Sr. Mary de Paul Sullivan

Sr. Mary Placidus Sullivan

Sr. Mary Holy Cross Welch

HISTORY: The Sisters of Charity of Cincinnati were founded by Mother Elizabeth Seton in 1809 at Emmitsburg, Maryland. Envisioning the need in America for a community with the spirit of the Daughters of Charity of St. Vincent de Paul in France, Elizabeth Bayley Seton, an American convert, was inspired to establish such a congregation in America. In 1829, in answer to an appeal of Bishop Fenwick, four of

(Illustration reference # 9)   these Sisters left Emmitsburg to open an orphanage in Cincinnati. This little group was the nucleus of what, in 1851, became an independent Community, the Sisters of Charity of Cincinnati. The 1400 members serve the Church in Colorado, Illinois, Maryland, Michigan, New Mexico, Ohio, and in China.

PURPOSE: The life work of the Sister of Charity is the sanctification of her own soul and the salvation of the souls of others. Today the Sisters operate a college for young women, academies for girls, a boy's military academy, day nurseries, grade and high schools. Their zeal for souls takes them to labor in home and foreign missions; to care for the sick, the deaf, the foundling and the orphan; to conduct vacation schools; to work among the poor and suffering in social centers, and in broken homes.

QUALIFICATIONS:

*   An applicant should be between 16 and 28 years of age, of sound mind and good health, and of good character.

*   Especially should she have a desire to glorify God, to sanctify her soul, and to spend her life for the salvation of the souls of others.

HABIT: The Sisters wear a black habit with a round black cape covering the shoulders and extending below the waist. They wear a white guimpe and a white cap covered by a black veil, which is somewhat longer than the cape.

It was during Eastertide that the call came for these Sister of Ohio. Every experienced nurse was sent by their Superior into war service. Six went to Camp Dennison, fifteen miles from Cincinatti, Ohio with magdeline Cooper as their German intepreter. Eight were received in Cincinatti where they worked in old waehouses turned hospital. Others arrived at Pawpaw, Virginia at Cumberland Hospital; Camp Dennison, St. Joseph'sHospital in in Cincinatti, and Baltimore, Marylands Mountain City hospital; Saint John's Hospital near Cincinatti; Wheeling West Virginia's

Military Hospitals and the State Hospital in Nashville, Tennessee among others.

They also tended the wounded and ill aboard floating hospitals near Shilo during the end of the battle and after until the last patient was taken from the vacinity. They worked in hotels, warehouses, large barns and tents that were converted to hospitals near many battlefields.

Sister Anthony was said to have known many of the great generals of the war and to have dined with the President of the Southern States on several occassions. [18] Below are the known names of those brave Siters that answered the call of the Nation.

Mother Josephine Harvey

Sr. Anthony O'Connell	Sr. Gabriella Crowe
Sr. Basilia Applegate	Sr. Cleophas Cummins
Sr. Augusta Barron	Sr. Winifred Cummins
Sr. Louise Barron	Sr. Constantia Dolan
Sr. Cephas Bray	Sr. Laurence Donaher
Sr. Benedicta Cain.	Sr. Clement Doyle
Sr. Clotilda Cain	Sr. Philomena Erwin
Sr. Magdalen Cooper	Sr. Theodosia Farran
Sr. Stanislaus Ferris	Sr. Mary Garvin
Sr. Sophia Gillmeyer	Sr. Jane Garvin
Sr. Aiphonsa Gordon	Sr. Beatrice Hastings
Sr. Ann Joseph Hughes	Sr. Bernardine King
Sr. Dominica Lavan	Sr. Mary Ignatia Mulcahy
Sr. Ann Cecilia McDonald.	Sr. Euphrasia McGary
Sr. Seraphine McGrane	Sr. Eugenia McMullen
Sr. Camilla O'Mara	Sr. Dominica Lavan
Sr. Mary Ignatia Mulcahy	Sr. Ann Cecilia McDonald.
Sr. Euphrasia McGary	Sr. Seraphine McGrane
Sr. Eugenia McMullen	Sr. Camilla O'Mara
Sr. Agnes Phillips	Sr. Veronica Phillips
Sr. Ambrosia Schwartz	Sr. Gonzaga Sheehan

---

[18] Jolly, Ellen Ryan; *"nuns of the Battlefield"*.

Sisters of Charity - New York City

HISTORY: The Sisters of Charity of the Archdiocese of New York were founded by Mother Elizabeth Seton at Emmitsburg, Maryland, in 1809. In 1817,at the request of Bishop Connolly of New York, Mother Seton sent Sisters to care for the needy dependent children of that diocese. In 1847, the Separate New York Motherhouse was established. The great city, with its throngs of children, its poverty and sickness, its demands for Catholic education on all levels, has for nearly one hundred and fifty years held out appealing hands to these Sisters, who have always responded gladly with sacrifice and service. The Community works include a college, academies, elementary and high schools, hospitals, and homes for dependent children. The Sisters carry on extensive missionary activities also among the natives of the Bahama Islands.

PURPOSE: The Purpose of the Community is to promote the glory of God by the sanctification of its members, by the apostolate of Catholic education and by the service of the poor through the spiritual and corporal works of mercy. The Sisters take perpetual vows.

QUALIFICATIONS:
* Age limits are 17 to 30. * Candidates must have an earnest desire to serve God faithfully in the religious life. * Because the Community works provide opportunities for all types of service, no special degree of education is stipulated as a requirement for entrance.

HABIT: The distinguishing marks of the costume of the New York Sisters are the cape and cap such as were worn by Mother Seton. The habit is black with a white collar and white undersleeves. The cap is of black silk. A large rosary hangs from the belt.

On Sept 9,1862 the Hon. Edwin Stanton, Secretary of War, formally requested the help of the Black-Cap Sisters of New York. They began their work at St. Joseph Hospital formerly a military academy where Sister Ulrica nursed to health the son of Captain William Seaton of the United States Navy and grandson of Mother Seaton (the foundress of the New York Sisters of Charity). The names of these Sisters are as follows:

Sr. Mary Perpetua Frumgoole   Sr. Mary Emerenta Hanaway
Sr. Mary Antoinette Kelly   Sr. Mary Columba Lawrence
Sr. Mary Assisium Madden   Sr. Mary Teresa McCloskey
Sr. Mary Justine McGlynn   Sr. Mary Francesca Molitor
Sr. Mary Christine Myers   Sr. Mary Ann Celia Nealis
Sr. Mary Ulrica O'Reilly   Sr. Mary Scholastica Wuinn
Sr. Mary Rosina Wightman

Sisters of Charity—of Nazareth

HISTORY: The Congregation of the Sisters of Charity of Nazareth was established near Bardstown, Kentucky, in December, 1812. Father J. B. David, later Bishop of Mauricastro, and Catherine Spalding, the first Superior, are regarded as co-Founders of the Community which now numbers approximately 1450 members. The name, Sisters of Charity of Nazareth, was chosen because the founders planned that the Sisters would devote themselves to varied works of charity. Schools were soon opened and through the years new works have been undertaken whenever the need arose and Sisters were available. Sisters of Charity of Nazareth are engaged in the works of the Congregation in ninety branch houses located in the Archdiocese of Boston, Louisville, and Washington, D. C., and in eleven dioceses. The Sisters of Charity of Nazareth take the three vows of Poverty, Chastity, and Obedience.

PURPOSE: Mother Catherine personally initiated many of the multiform works, which include: primary, elementary, and high school teaching in parochial schools and academies; higher education in colleges and in nurses' training schools; care of the sick in hospitals, mental as well as physical; care of orphans and summer camps for girls. Schools for negro pupils have been conducted since 1871, and Sisters have been engaged in educational and hospital work in Patna, India, since 1947.

QUALIFICATIONS: The chief qualifications for candidates are:
*good will, good judgment, good health
*age: 16-30 (exceptions are sometimes made for suitable candidates over 30)
*entrance dates Jan. 18, June 7, and Sept. 24
*candidates are expected to present the usual customary canonical certificates.

HABIT: The habit is black and includes a circular cape, apron, and a white cap.

Early in 1861 the Sisters offered their services to minister as nurses in government hospitals. They began their service at Louivelle, Kentucky in three large manufacturing buildings converted to hospitals. And Bardstown at the Baptist College. They also filled pressing need for their services in Calhoun's two Protestant churches; Pasucah's Marine Hospital and Baptist church turned hospital; Lousiville's General Hospital; Lexington's Confederate Hospital and Transylvania College Hospital; as well as hospitals in Owensboro. They also worked on the battlefields of Shilo.

One story of these Sisters is that a faithful black servant within the Paducah Hospital was asked whether the Sisters' sympathies lie with the Union or Confederacy, the woman replied: "De Sisters dey ain't for de Noff nuh de Souf; dey's for God"[19] Thus attesting to her degree of prudence and fidelity as well as the Sisters' non-partisan stand.

At times their hospitals were surrounded by the efforts of battle and not once did they leave their posts until the last patient was evacuated. Below are the only known names of the leigon of "White Cap" Sisters on file in Washington, D.C.

Sr. Mary Blanch Traynor, Superior

Sr. Mary Gaudentia Beatie	Sr. Mary Peter Brady
Sr. Mary Angela Brooks	Sr. Mary Ida Brophy
Sr. Mary Dominica Byrne	Sr. Mary Mark Byrne
Sr. Mary Sophia Curton	Sr. Mary Lucy Dosh
Sr. Mary Regina Drumm	Sr. Mary Martha Drury
Sr. Mary Humbaline Fagan	Sr. Mary Scolastica Fenwick
Sr. Mary Patricia Grymes	Sr. Mary Clarence Hanley
Sr. Mary Vincent Hardie	Sr. Mary Louis Hines
Sr. Mary Joseph Hollihand	Sr. Mary Erminilda Kelly
Sr. Mary de Chantal Kenny	Sr. Mary Justine Linnehan
Sr. Mary Alexia Highon	Sr. Mary Cathrine Malone
Sr. Mary Constatia Malone	Sr. Mary Appolomia McGill
Sr. Mary Borromeo McKenny	Sr. Mary Phillipa Pollock
Sr. Mary Placida Sisness	Sr. Mary Mildred Travers

These Sisters are one of the twelve representative Sisters portrayed on the monument erected in their honor in Washington, D.C.

---

[19] Jolly, Ellen Ryan; *"Nuns of the Battlefield"*

HISTORY: Frances Schervier was the Foundress of the Sisters of The Poor of St. Francis, a Congregation devoted to charitable work among the sick poor. Born in Aachen, Germany, she came from a pious Catholic family of excellent economic and social position. Devout from childhood, she was particularly taken with Christ's injunction about providing for His poor. Her friend, Gertrude Frank, had a vision in which Frances was commanded to found a congregation. The Congregation originated in 1845 with five women. They were called upon for various types of service, mainly the care of the sick poor in hospitals. The American branch of the congregation was founded in 1858.

PURPOSE: Though the principal work of the Community is the care of the poor in hospitals, the Sisters are not all nurses. All talents can be used in the Congregation. There is need for Sisters as technicians, dieticians, bookkeepers, secretaries, for household and many other domestic duties.

QUALIFICATIONS: The principal requisites for admission are:
*age: 15-30
*an earnest desire for personal sanctification
*legitimate birth, good reputation
*free from sickness, deformity and from debt
*possession of sound judgment.

HABIT: The Sisters wear a brown habit and scapular, on which is embroidered a red cross with the crown of thorns---on the right hand a plain gold ring. The veil is black.

In early November, 11861 they conducted three large Marine Hospitals in Cincinatti; four Sister's Hospital in Columus, Ohio; Covington Hospital in Kentucky; and aboard a steamer ship turned floating hospital. They worked with steel and compasion in the surgical areas as weell os on the wards. Their administrative ability proved what just a handful of Sisters could do with the large responsibilities placed upon them. These then are the recorded names of those few with such large responsibilities.

Sr. Mary Tobia Baur
Sr. Mary Felicitas Dorst
Sr. Mary Antonia Goeb
Sr. Mary Innocentia Koch
Sr. Mary Anna Oeschner

Sr. Mary Aegidia Conde
Sr. Mary Magdalen Feeny
Sr. Mary Stylita Jergens
Sr. Mary Eusebia Mertens

HISTORY: The Sisters of Third Order of Preachers, more commonly known as the Dominican Sisters, were organized toward the middle of the thirteenth century in Europe. Following the rule of St. Dominican, these sisters grew in numbers as they spread throughout the world manifesting zeal in courage and contemplation as they sought to sanctify themselves and extend the kingdom of God. Over one hundred years ago this spirit arose in the United States when the first community of Dominican Sisters was founded in this country. Nine valiant young women began the Dominican way of life in what was to become St. Catharine, Kentucky, the oldest and mother community of many Dominican foundations in the United States.

PURPOSE: The Dominican Sisters of St. Catharine are primarily engaged in teaching in the various levels of education extending from the university to the grammar school level. The sisters also devote themselves to the spiritual and physical work of caring for the suffering in four hospitals.

QUALIFICATIONS: Young girls interested in following the Dominican way of life as a Sister of St. Catharine of Sienna should:
    * possess good health with no physical defects
*good character
*be ready and willing to accept any duty to which they may be assigned.

On October 8th, 1862 Generals Bragg amd Buell fought a most desperate battle almost at the door of St. Cathrine's Convent. Despite this not once during that battle nor during the four long years of war did the Dominican Sisters receive the slightest offense from any soldier. Many stories of their adventures with soldiers always afoot can be read in the books written prior to this and make very interesting reading. Suffice it to say that the Sisters fed and cared for many soldiers on their own grounds many times. Everything the Sisters possesed was at the disposal of the soldier.

They came to the battlefield of Perryville and administered to those wounded and dying there under the protection of Bragg's troops. They gave water to the soldiers as they administered to their bodily and spiritual needs and attended the surgeons at the operating tables. The following are the names that have been recorded:

Sr. Mary Teresa Caho

Sr. Mary Clement

Sr. Mary Francois Coppe

Sr. Mary Rose Fennelly

Sr. Mary Catharine Kidwell

Sr. Mary Agnes Maguire

Sr. Mary Aquin Montgomery

Sr. Mary Vallina Montgomery

Sr. Mary Regina O'Meara

Sr. Mary Benven Rumph

Sr. Mary Columba Walsh

Sr. Mary Thomas Wight

Sr. Mary Celcilia Carey

Sr. Mary Rachel Conway

Sr. Mary Magdalene Edelen

Sr. Mary Francis Kennedy

Sr. Mary Angela Lynch

Sr. Mary Josephine Meagher

Sr. Mary Imelda Montgomery

Sr. Mary Ann O'Brien

Sr. Mary Margaret Queen

Sr. Mary Augusta Thomas

Sr. Mary Helen Whelan

Sr. Mary Catharine Young

History: In the spring of 1860, shortly before the outbreak of the Civil War, the Most Reverend James Whelan, O. P., Bishop of Nashville, applied to St. Mary's Convent, Somerset, Ohio, for a number of sisters to conduct a school for girls in the city of Nashville. Four sisters were assigned to this new responsibility and in October 1860, the pioneers in the southland opened St. Cecilia Academy. Soon after the arrival of the sisters, the Civil War broke out, and battles raged within the immediate vicinity. In spite of financial losses and other hardships, the sisters carried on their work of teaching. At present, the Sisters of the St. Cecilia Congregation conduct eighteen schools in the Nashville Diocese; two in the Diocese of Richmond and one each in the Archdioceses of Chicago and Cincinnati. The congregation is of Pontifical status, its constitutions were approved by Pope Pius XII June 14, 1948.

PURPOSE: The principal end of the congregation is the sanctification of its members through the observance of the three simple vows of Poverty, Chastity and Obedience, the Rule of St. Augustine and the approved Constitutions. The special end is the Christian education of youth in institutions of learning and any other educational or charitable work undertaken by the congregation with the permission of its superiors.

QUALIFICATIONS:

* Applicants over 30 years of age require the consent of the General Council for admission. Before being admitted to temporary profession novices must have completed their 16th year.

* Candidates for admission to the novitiate are required to present certificates of Baptism and Confirmation, a letter of recommendation from their pastor or some other priest and a health certificate.

HABIT: The Sisters of the St. Cecilia Congregation wear the white and black habit of the Order of St. Dominic. The novices wear a white veil, the professed sisters a black veil.

As of the writing of this book the Convent of Memphis Tennessee is no longer on our roles. However, Nashville Tennessee also has a Convent and information may be obtained there.

After the battle of Belmont on November 7th, 1861 the Cathedral was turned into a makeshift hospital and the Sisters from St. Agnes Convent were enlisted to nurse the soldiers brought there. When Nashville was later taken, the hospital was moved to Memphis and patients were transferred there. After the battles of Shilo and Pittsburg Landing, trainloads of soldiers were brought to Memphis. The Sisters also worked on the field of Perryville and Shilo. The following Sisters' names were written in the National records when the Federal Government took Memphis. All others were lost.

Sr. Mary Louise Caine
Sr. Mary Francis Conlon
Sr. Mary Rosalie Gonzague
Sr. Mary Bernard Madigan
Sr. Mary Magdalen McKernan
Sr. Mary Thomas O'Meara
Sr. Mary Alberta Rumph
Sr. Mary Imelda Spangler

Sr. Mary Magdalen Clark
Sr. Mary Pius Fitzpatrick
Sr. Mary Ann Hanlon
Sr. Mary Joseph McKernan
Sr. Mary Vincent Nicholas
Sr. Mary Veronica Ray
Sr. Mary Ann Simpson
Sr. Mary Josephine Whelan

Father Ryan, the soldier, poet, priest of the South, wrote many poems during his time working with the soldiers. While "*The Conquered Banner*" was written in his heart's blood while he was stationed at Knoxville, Tennessee, "*Reunited*" was a hymn of gratitude.

The Conquered Banner
Furl that banner, softly slowly,
Treat it gently – it is holy;
For it droops above the dead.
Touch it no – unfold it never,
Let it drop there, furled forever,
For its people's hopes are dead.

Reunited
No hand might clasp from land to land –
Yea – thee was one to bridge the tide;
For at the touch of Mercy's hand,
The North and South stood side by side;
The Bride of Snow, The Bride of Sun,
In Charity's espousls, were made one.

HISTORY: The Congregation of the Sisters of St. Joseph, which now numbers over 30,000 members, was founded in Le Puy, France, in 1650, by the Right Reverend Bishop Henry de Maupas and Rev. John Peter Medaille S.J. Disbanded during the French Revolution, it was later reorganized by Mother St. John Fontbonne, who had escaped death in the Reign of Terror, at St. Etienne in 1808. The first Motherhouse originated in Lyons under her authority in 1816. In 1836, upon the request of Most Reverend Joseph Rosati, the first Bishop of St. Louis, she sent six Sisters to establish the first foundation in the United States. There are at present 24 independent Motherhouses in the United States, (with the exception of the Sisters of St. Joseph of Carondolet who are a Pontifical Institute), whose immediate Superior is the Bishop of the diocese in which they are located.

PURPOSE: The general purpose of the Sisters of St. Joseph is the glory of God through the personal sanctification of its members by means of the three simple vows. The special purpose and their most extensive work is the instruction of youth from kindergarten to college; managing hospitals, charitable institutions, orphanages, schools for the deaf, homes for the aged, as well as other works of charity.

QUALIFICATIONS: Young Catholic women may be accepted who:
*are under 30
*are imbued with the desire to give glory to God

HABIT: The habit is made quite simply of black serge, with full skirt and sleeves. A guimpe and cornette of white linen, a black rosary, and a soft veil covering the face complete the religious garb.

Wheeling, Virginia, because of its unique geographical location, felt the repercussions of each battle from both sides. Patients arrived hourly by ambulance, cattle trains and transport boats. The Sisters of St. Joseph cheerfully took more than their quota of patients and earned theeir nickname, the "Angels of the Wards". The Wheeling Hospital the Sisters had established in 1856, was already a well established and respected hospital. The Mother Superior, Mother Immaculate Feeney, was ideal for her position as Superintendant because of her many years of study and experience in war work in her homeland of Ireland.

In February of 1864, her health failing rapidly, Mother Feeny was forced to resign her position. Barely had the replacement, Mother Mary de Chantal, arrived from New York when a request for nurses came. Groups of Sisters were sent forth to White Sulfur Springs, Virginia. The Sisters often slept in quiet corners of wardrooms because there were so many wounded and so few of the Sisters.

While the Northern soldiers and Southern soldiers fought outside the hospital, within it they were at peace. Such was the influence of the Sisters of St. Joseph.

These are the Sisters of Wheeling, West Virginia whose names are written in the archives of Washington, D.C.:

Mother Mary de Chantal Keating

Sr. Mary Evangelist Breslin	Sr. Mary Ignatius Farley
Sr. Mary Immaculate Feeney	Sr. Mary Joseph Whelan
Sr. Mary Stanislaus Matthews	Sr. Mary Stanislaus Honan
Sr. Mary Agnes Kelly	Sr. Mary Vincent Smythe
Sr. Mary Aloysius Sullivan	

The Sisters of St. Joseph at Philadelphia, Pennsyvania often worked far afield from their Convent. On land, floating hospitals, camps and many fields of combat they tended to soldiers who were sick at heart as well as body. Unforunately very little was written about the particulars of their service. They did establish the St. Joseph's Hospital in Philadelphia prior to 1859 and it was there they received many patients. They also took charge of the soldiers in Harrisburg at both Camp Curtin and at the Church Hospital. In April of 1862 they took charge on the floating hospitals, *"The Wilden"*, *"The Commodore"* and *"The Mount"*. The roster of the United States Army reads as follows:

Mother Mary Saint John Fournier

Sr. Mary Mt. Carmel Egan	Sr. Mary Felix Haverty
Sr. Mary Anselm Jennings	Sr. Mary John Kieran
Sr. Mary Philomena Maher	Sr. Mary Bruno McMahon
Sr. Mary Constantina McMenamin	Sr. Mary Laurentia O'Donnell
Sr. Mary Camillus Phelan	Sr. Mary Monica Pue
Sr. Mary Ignatius Ryan	Sr. Mary Xavier alker
Sr. Mary Patrick Ward	

HISTORY: In 1829, the Most Reverend John England, first Bishop of Charleston, South Carolina, realized he needed assistance in caring for the orphans and the little slave children of his diocese. Accordingly, he sought for help. Three young women, originally from Ireland, came from Baltimore to aid Bishop England in the work of his vast missionary diocese which then comprised three States, the Carolinas and Georgia. This was the beginning of the Congregation of the Sisters of Charity of Charleston, founded under the patronage of Our Lady of Mercy. In 1835, the growing Congregation joined in the fight against the devastating yellow fever epidemic in which many Nuns sacrificed their own lives while endeavoring to save the lives of others. The War between the States saw many of the Sisters nursing the wounded of both armies. Since those early days the Congregation has opened schools, hospitals, social service centers, an orphanage, and catechetical centers, in South Carolina and in New Jersey.

PURPOSE: The purpose of the Congregation is to glorify God and sanctify its members by the practice of the spiritual and corporal works of mercy according to the Rule of the Sisters of Charity (St. Vincent de Paul). Their principal works are teaching and nursing the sick.

QUALIFICATIONS: Young women between the ages of 16 and 30 are eligible to join this Congregation provided that they:
are in good health
have a docile, sociable disposition
desire to serve God in the religious life

HABIT: The habit is made of black woolen material. A white collar completes a circular cape which extends a little below the waist. An apron of the same material as the habit covers the habit completely in front. The head is covered by a close-fitting white cap over which is worn a white bonnet covered by a black veil.

When the first guns were heard at half past four o'clock on April 12, 1861, Charelston's Sister-nurses entered at once upon their heart-breaking duties. With thirty years of experience these nurses knew full well what horrors those first shots would mean.

The Ropen Military Hospital was among the first post-hospitals to be established in Charelston. Between thirty and thirty-five Sisters were on duty at Ropen and its scores of affiliated tent hospitals. Many Sisters also seved at White Sulphur Springs Military Hospital, Virginia, and on July 10th, 1863, during the second seige of Charleston, the Convent was turned into another hospital to receive the over-flow of wounded and dying.

Many of the Sisters' names were lost or never recorded. Below are the few that were retrieved:

Mother mary Theresa Barry

Sr,. Mary Isidore Barry	Sr. Mary de Sales Brennan
Sr. Mary Veronica Carney	Sr. Mary Ignatius Clarke
Sr. Mary de Chantal Cleary	Sr. Mary Stanislaus Coventry
Sr. Mary Xavier Dune	Sr. Mary Bernard Frank
Sr. Mary Vincent Jones	Sr. Mary Francis Kyte
Sr. Mary Helena Marlow	Sr. Mary Alphonsus Moore
Sr. Mary Agatha McNamara	Sr. Mary Ann O'Dowd
Sr. Marymartha O'Gorman	Sr. Mary Peter O'Sullivan
Sr. Mary Evangilist Smith	

HISTORY: The Sisters of Providence from Ruille, France, came to Saint Mary-of-the-Woods on October 22, 1840. Leading the six missionaries was Mother Theodore Guerin---an educator decorated by the French Government, and the only religious to whom the Ruille Superiors would confide the American foundation. Within a year the Sisters had begun their work of educating young girls, by opening what was to become the first chartered women's college in Indiana; within five years, they had laid the framework of their present widespread system of education. Today in that system, some 1400 Sisters teach 40,000 children in kindergartens, grade schools, secondary schools, and two colleges---in five archdioceses and 11 dioceses.

PURPOSE: The Congregation honors Divine Providence by "a great zeal for the glory of God, an ardent desire to acquire perfection, and to contribute to the sanctification of their neighbor." This is done through teaching and such supplementary activities as secretarial work, nursing, technical, and domestic positions.

QUALIFICATIONS: The applicant:

* Must be the offspring of legitimate marriage.

* Should have completed her fifteenth year.

* Should have a serious, cheerful, agreeable character; good health; ability to be trained for teaching or a supplementary duty.

* Makes a 2½ year novitiate, then takes vows---temporary, then perpetual---of Poverty, Chastity, and Obedience

HABIT: Simplicity of line and design characterizes the black wool habit, white linen neckerchief and headdress, black veil, and chaplet. A white crucifix, worn suspended from the neck, completes the garb.

They served at the Indianapolis Military Hospital and in a hospital of tents near Vincennes. Though they did not stray far from home, they saw more than five-thousand Confederate soldier pass through their doors. They treated each no differently than they did the Union soldiers. Below is a list of their names.

Sr. Mary Rose Donaghue	Sr. Mary Felix Buchanan
Sr. Mary Sophie Glenn	Sr. Mary Athanasius Fogarty
Sr. Mary Eugenia Gorman	Sr. Mary Francis Guthneck
Sr. Mary Mathilda Swimley	Sr. Mary Frances Ann Carney
Sr. Mary Henrietta McKenzie	Sr. Mary Louise Maloney
Sr. Mary Helena Burns	

HISTORY: In 1825, the Reverend Charles F. Boutelou, a zealous French priest of St. Francis de Paule in Tours, France, conceived the idea of uniting a number of young ladies as tertiaries of Our Lady of Mount Carmel (Carmelites). This noble project formed the nucleus for the first chapter of the history of the Congregation of the Sisters of Our Lady of Mount Carmel. The Revolution of 1830, aimed primarily at the destruction of the Church in France, forced the growing Community to disperse. Father Boutelou sought refuge in Louisiana. Upon his arrival in New Orleans he told Bishop de Nekere of the plight of the Sisters. The Bishop invited them to his diocese. Mother Theresa Chevreul and Mother St. Augustine Clerc eagerly volunteered. With the zeal of a St. Theresa and the love of an Augustine they planted the seed which developed through the years. Today the Sisters conduct eleven elementary schools and six high schools in the Archdiocese of New Orleans and the Diocese of Lafayette, Louisiana. Within a year they are to open their first hospital in the city of Thibodaux, Louisiana.

PURPOSE: The primary purpose of the Congregation of the Sisters of Our Lady of Mount Carmel is the sanctification of its members by the observance of the simple vows of Poverty, Chastity, and Obedience. The secondary object is the Christian education of youth and the care of the sick.

QUALIFICATIONS:

Young ladies and widows, between the ages of 15 and 30, may be admitted into the Congregation, provided they possess a true vocation based on supernatural motives.

Postulancy---six months; novitiate---two years; following a period of three years, the Sister makes Perpetual Vows.

Candidates provide their own clothing and defray the expenses of the Novitiate, besides providing a small dowry.

Poverty is no hindrance to acceptance.

The Sisters left their teaching work to nurse the soldiers on October 27, 1862. They began an emergency hospital atLabadieville, Louisiana following a fight over a bridge outside of that town, Here the Sisters began their brave journey into a future of war. Instead of going to the battle as their Northern Sisters did, the battles came to them. They were seen on many battlefields around New Orleans and were caught in artists' depictions of the war.

They shared all that they had with soldiers on both sides of the conflict. They also shared every deprivation with the soldiers and with those poor of the city. They following names are written on the military roll of honor.

Mother Saint Patrick Heffernan

Sr. du Carmel Giroir	Sr. Saint Bernard Guerin
Sr. Saint John Baptist Ligier	Sr. Mary Albertine Passon
Sr. Mary Louise Pelen	Sr. Mary Bridget Phelan
Sr. Mary Magdalen Seely	Sr. Mary Veronica

HISTORY: The Order of St. Ursula, founded by Angela Merici in Brescia, Italy, in 1535, was the first group of women in the Church to be dedicated to the teaching of girls. The Ursulines of the Congregation of Paris were formed in 1572; from this Congregation the Venerable Mary of the Incarnation became the first woman missionary to settle in Quebec, 1639; likewise, in 1727 a group of French Ursulines landed in New Orleans to found the first Catholic School for girls in America. During the fall of the year 1900 over 100 Ursuline Congregations, which are being augmented yearly, from all over the world united to form the Roman Union of Ursulines. The Ursuline Order, of which there are a few independent Motherhouses existing in the United States, founded the first Catholic college for Women in the State of New York at New Rochelle in 1904. PURPOSE: The Ursulines, who take the three simple vows, have from their very beginning been engaged in teaching. By means of a personal and social formation in a Catholic family atmosphere, Ursulines through the centuries have prepared thoroughly Catholic women for the Church and society in parochial schools, academies, and colleges in all parts of the world and in missions in Asia, Africa, South America, and Alaska.

QUALIFICATIONS:* Completion of high school; some college work is recommended. * Health and the ability to fulfill the obligations of the Ursuline life. * Girls may enter as teachers or as coadjutrix Sisters, who spend their lives in prayer and the auxiliary services essential to education. * All have the same probation, pronounce the same vows and enjoy in common all the spiritual and temporal benefits. * In the Ursulines of the Roman Union a tertianship of six months is made in Rome about ten years after the first Profession

HABIT: The Sisters of the Roman Union wear a black habit and veil fastened by a cincture; white is worn in the tropics. The Ursulines of Paris wear a black habit with a long trailing Church mantle and a leather cincture of St. Augustine.

The Ursulines have had a long history of nursing during wars in the United States since their establishment in New Orleans in 1639. The first of which as early as September 14, 1759 when Generals Montcalm and Wolfe faced each other on thePplains of Abraham. Here they turned their Convent into a military Hospital to care for the wounded and dying.

Half a century later they nursed the soldiers again during the seige of New Orleans on the eigth of January, 1815. To tell of their heroism in detail during the time between 1861 and 1865 would take a greata many pages and could well fill a separate book. Suffice it to say that no soldier was ever turned away. When the city was beseiged, they stayed behind to nurse the wounded despite the offers of transport to safety.

Several diaries relate soldiers stories of the Sisters work on battlefields. They were often seen on the battle lines caring for wounded, heedless of the danger around them.

They helped to establish hospitals outside of the city in order to help protect their patients from the constant bombardment of New orleans and Galvaston Island. Both invader and defender were cared for on equal terms as were the negro soldiers.

They took charge of all wounds that were not to be surgically treated and helped with the surgeries as well.

While many records were lost in the last days of the Confederacy, through fire and vandalism, the names of a handful of Sisters are known. Their gravestones are still decorated today by members of the Grand Army of the Republic and the Sons of Confederate Veterans. They are:

Mother Saint Pierre Harington
Sr. Saint Anne Stohl
Sr. Mary Anastasia Goux
Sr. Mary Ambrose Bennett
Sr. Saint mary Nolte
Sr. Saint Ursula Prenard

Sisters of St. Brigid

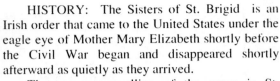

HISTORY: The Sisters of St. Brigid is an Irish order that came to the United States under the eagle eye of Mother Mary Elizabeth shortly before the Civil War began and disappeared shortly afterward as quietly as they arrived.

The common spelling of the name is St. Bridget though the documentation shows clearly the spelling is St. Brigid. In the end suffice it to say we are speaking (Illustration Reference # 20) of the Irish St. Brigid rather than the Scandinavian St. Bridget.

St. Brigid founded her order in the 5th century A. D. in County Kildare, Ireland. She was a pioneer in the education of women, giving of food to the poor, and healing of the sick. Her story is an interesting one and can be read in it's intirety in *These Splendid Sisters* by James J. Walsh.

St. Brigid was an abbess of an institution with both men and women under her jurisdiction and achieved a place not only in Irish hearts, but in those of many countries whom her missionaries have touched, including the Americas. It is said that the people all over the world celebrated her feast day for well over a thousand years.

While this order is very real and as most orders not named here, would have done much to succor the ill and injured soldiers that crossed their path. So, many of you wonder why I chose to add this order to our list. Much of my research shows that while not all Orders or Communities contributed in a way that would have been documented in sources available to us today, they none the less contributed a great deal. "The Religious Sister of every Order hurried forth where danger was greatest and the needs of the body and soul most pressing. Their companions at home were performing ...fourfold the work"[20] in hospitals, asylums, orphanages, schools and pest houses.

They continued to run the orphanages, the schools, the houses for the insane, and visit the prisons. They often cared for wounded or ill soldiers that crossed their paths briefly. They gave bread and water to those traveling past their work and living quarters, very often giving all they had leaving little for themselves.

Their selfless dedication to humanity no matter what their uniform or skin color earned them the respect of both armies. The Sisters often crossed lines between the North and South without challenge, so great was

---

[20] Jolly, Ellen Ryan; *"The Nuns of the Battlefield"*

the trust in them. It is to all of those Sisters not named by other sources that I dedicate these few pages. The Sisters of St. Brigid was chosen as a representative Order because of the selfless dedication to healing they instill in their Community. Their sense of wonder and awe of the goodness of Christ shows in their charity works.

Many of these Sisters were far from their homelands of France, Germany, Ireland, and England while others born in the United States watched as their homeland was torn apart with the strife.

It is with this that I present to you the creation of a national organization of women who portray Civil War Sisters. They all come under the heading of Sisters of St. Brigid. They are dedicated to teaching the public about the role of Nuns and portraying their roles as accurately as possible. At this writing there are a great many members across the United States of America. (See Chapter seven for a listing of contacts in your area)

Girls must be 14 to pose as a postulate and 16 to pose as a novice or above. To wear the black veil, the candidate must prove herself on battlefield and in testing of knowledge.

Below are the names I was able to find of the Sisters at the Motherhouse in Southern Missouri:

Mother Superior Mother Mary Elizabeth

Sr. Mary Virginia

Sr. Mary Theresa

Sr. Mary Joan

Sr. Mary Henritta

Sr. Mary Lorena

Sr. Mary Joephine

Chapter 4

The Beliefs of the Church

A critical part of reenacting is knowing your subject well. This chapter will explore an area unfamiliar to the non-Catholic population. This is an incredibly condensed version of their beliefs is not intended to be the only research you do in this area. There is not enough room in this book for more than the briefest of information, however, this will get you started in the right direction.

The Church, founded by Christ, has an actual birth date as the day of Pentecost. Witnessing and maintaining faith is all important in this religion. Of the three methods of doing this, Prayer is the most important. Through prayer a communion with God and a greater understanding of the blessed trinity and of faith is reached. Constant prayer gives strength to one's belief.

There are four types of prayer practiced. The Divine office a group of prayers of the Church. This consists of prayers during Mass and those that are required thorough out the year. The Profession of Faith (Creed), Our Father, and Eucharistic Prayers are all parts of this group.

The second group consists of the Rosary (prayers to Blessed Mother). These are prayers in preparation as well as the prayers in the recitation of the Rosary. The Creed and Our Father are included with other prayers such as Hail Mary, and Glory Be.

The third group of prayer is less structured. For God said: "Be still and know I am God". This is more of a meditative prayer not taken lightly as it is a one on one talk with God. The asking of Affections (short prayers from the heart), Petitions (requests for help from God) and Resolutions (practical plans for changing your life with God's help) are all parts of this prayer time.

The final group of Prayers reawaken the recognition that Christ alone is the light to the world. Meditation on scriptures and inspirational writings are the core of this type of prayer and form the base of the subject matter. This prayer is meant to help spiritual growth.

A Catholic receives Grace through the sacraments of church. Through frequent participation in mass, sacraments of penance and Eucharist, the resolve is strengthened to be faithful witness to Christ.

And finally the Teachings of Christ proclaim the primacy of the Light. Is the Alpha and Omega of the faith.

Beliefs

Catholics believe the soul has free will. That God is the ultimate reality. That You are bound to God even as you seek him and that God seeks you even as he has already found you through your baptism.

God communicates himself through revelations, doctrines and dogmas (scriptures). That God is three divine persons: The Father as the Creator, The Son as the Savior and The Holy Spirit as the Sanctifier. To further clarify any of the information in this chapter start with the Handbook for Today's Catholic.

Then there are gifts of the Spirit. Gifts of the first kind are intended for sanctification of the person receiving them. They are permanent supernatural qualities and tune the person in with inspirations of the Holy Spirit. These can include things like wisdom, understanding, counsel, fortitude, knowledge, piety, and fear of the Lord.

Gifts of the second kind called charismas, are extraordinary favors and are granted for the help of others. These can include speaking with wisdom, speaking with knowledge, faith, healing, miracles, prophecy, discerning of spirits, tongues, interpreting speeches, etc.

In a state of Grace you have faith, hope, charity and love of god is bound with love of others.

Mary as the Mother of Jesus and of the Church is also Mother to us in the order of Grace. The Saints are people who served God and their neighbors in so outstanding a way that they have been canonized (declared that they are in heaven). They are held up as models and prayers to them are encouraged for intercession with God for us all.

Original Sin is seen as an abused freedom in the garden of Eden resulting in distortion of relationship between God and Man causing a division, pain, bloodshed, loneliness and death.

Personal Sin is committed by the individual contrary to God's laws. Venial sins are easily forgiven sins. Mortal Sin is the most serious sins.

Baptism and confirmation is seen as essential to receive the seal of the Holy Spirit. Penance is seen as a way toward reconciliation with Heaven. The Eucharist is a reenactment of the last supper with the wafer representing the body of Christ and the Wine representing the blood.

The Catholic faith also believes in Anointing of the sick. One need not be on the verge of death to receive this anointing.

Matrimony is seen as a Sacrament of life-giving oneness and is viewed as a great mystery. A couple lives a life of love deliberately and consciously because it is their vocation and by their closeness they affect others with something special. A couple's love gives life to other people. It is considered an insoluble and exclusive union.

Holy Orders is the special or ministerial priesthood of Christ that certain male members of the Church receive through the sacrament of holy orders. It is the conference of special character, an interior capability that empowers them to act in the person of Christ the head. They are specifically the Priests and Decons of the church who act in Christ's stead as head of the chirch. This being set apart is meant to help these people do God's work with total dedication.

Practices

The Catholic Church teaches its parishoners to follow God's two great Commandments: You shall love the Lord, your God, with all your heart, with all your soul and with all your mind; and you shall love your neighbor as yourself. The Commandments of God (you know, the usual TEN) are an extension of the two great commandments. They tell you how to love your God and Your neighbor.

Precepts of the Church are listed from time to time. These duties of Catholics change according to the times they live in. The following are traditionally mentioned Precepts: To keep the holy day of the Lord's Resurrection: to worship God by participating in mass every Sunday and every holy day of obligation; Lead a sacramental life; To observe the marriage laws of the Church; To strengthen and support the Church; To do penance, including abstaining from meat and fasting from food on the appointed days.

Holy Days of Obligation are special feasts on which Catholics who have reached the age of reason are seriously obliged to attend Mass and to avoid unnecessary work. These include Mary Mother of God (Jan 1); Ascension Thursday (forty days after Easter); Mary's Assumption (Aug 15); All Saints' Day (Nov. 1) Mary's Immaculate Conception (Dec 8); Christmas Dec 25)

Regulations for Fast and Abstinence: all persons who have completed their seventh year are bound by the law of fast up to death or the loss of reason. This forbids the eating of red meats and allows only one full meal and two lighter meals in the course of the day and prohibits eating between meals. Ash Wednesday and Good Friday are also days of fast and abstinence and all other Fridays of Lent are days of abstinence only. Some form of penance is especially encouraged on all Fridays throughout the year.

Confession of Sins at least once a week is a reminder to receive the sacrament of penance on a regular basis. This is considered of great value as it makes one more deeply conformed to Christ and most submissive to the voice of the Spirit. After prayer and an examination of conscience to find out what sins you have committed, you enter the confessional.

The form for confession is as follows:

Father: greets you
You: respond and make the sign of the cross (touch the forehead, the chest, left shoulder then right shoulder) and say: In the name of the Father, and the Son, and the Holy Ghost, Amen".
Father: invites you to have confidence in God
You: "Bless me Father for I have sinned."
Father: reads or recites a short selection from the Bible.
You: tell how long it has been since your last confession. Then you tell your sins.
Father: gives you any necessary advice and answer your questions. After he assigns a penance you make an "Act of Contrition" (see the section on prayers).
Father then places his hands on your head (or extends is right hand toward you) and prays words of forgiveness. You will answer, "Amen".
Father then says "give thanks to the Lord, for he is good." you will answer:" His mercy endures for ever."
Father then dismisses you in these or similar words: "The Lord has freed you from your sins. Go in Peace."

How To Receive Communion

Holy Communion may be received on the tongue or in the hand and may be given under the form of bread alone or both bread and wine.

When the minister of the Eucharist addresses the communicant with the words "The Body of Christ," "The Blood of Christ," the communicant responds with "Amen" to each. When the minister raises the Eucharistic bread or wine, this is an invitation for the communicant to make an act of faith to express his or her belief in the Eucharist, to manifest a need and desire for the Lord, to accept the good news of Jesus' paschal mystery.

A clear, meaningful, and purposeful "Amen" is your response to this invitation. In this way you openly profess your belief in the presence of Christ in the Eucharistic bread and wine, as well as in his Body, the Church.

Liturgical Seasons of the Year

Advent: This season begins four weeks before Christmas. The Sunday which falls on or closest to November 30 is its starting point.

Christmas Season: This season lasts from Christmas until the Baptism of the Lord, the Sunday after Epiphany. The period from the end of Christmas Season until the beginning of Lent belongs to Ordinary Time.

Lent: The penitential season of Lent lasts forty days, beginning on Ash Wednesday and ending with the Mass of the Lord's Supper on Holy

Thursday. The final week is called Holy Week, and the last three days are called the Paschal Triduum.

Easter Season: This season, whose theme is resurrection from sin to the life of grace, lasts fifty days, from Easter to Pentecost.

Ordinary Time: This season comprises the thirty-three or thirty– four weeks in the course of the year that celebrate no particular aspect of the mystery of Christ. Instead, the mystery of Christ in all its fullness is celebrated. It includes not only the period between the end of the Christmas Season and the beginning of Lent but also all the Sundays after Pentecost to the last Sunday of the liturgical year.

Chapter 5

Rosary and Prayers

It is an important part of the role of a Catholic Nun that one should be well versed in the area of the Rosary and various Prayers. It is with this in mind that this chapter holds the most critical of the prayers and where available those prayers also in Latin and the method of praying the Rosary The *Latin* version will be in italics.

Prayers

Sign of the Cross—"In the name of the Father, and of the Son, and of the Holy Ghost. Amen" (said at the beginning and the end of prayers)

In Nomine, Patris, et Filii, et Spiritus Sancti. Amen.

Our Father—"Our Father, who art in heaven, hallowed be thy name; thy kingdom come; they will be done on earth as in heaven. Give us this day our daily bread; and forgive us our trespasses as we forgive those who trespass against us; and lead us not into temptation, but deliver us from evil. For thine is the kingdom, the power, and the glory, now and for ever. Amen."

Pater noster, qui es in coelis, sanctifier nomen tuum, adveniat regnum tuum, fiat vuluntas tua, sicut in coelo et in terra. Panem notsrom quotianum da nobis hodie. Et dimitte nobis debita nostra, sicut et nos dmittimus debitoribus. Et ne nos inducas in tentationem. Sed libera nos a malo. Amen

Hail Mary—"Hail Mary, full of grace. The Lord is with thee. Blessed art thou among women, and blessed is the fruit of thy womb, Jesus. Holy Mary, Mother of God, pray for us sinners, now and at the hour of our death. Amen."

Ave, Maria, gratia plena; Dominus tecum: benedicta tu in mulieriabus, et benedictus fructus ventris tui Jesus. Sancta Maria, Mater Dei, ora pro nobis peccatoribus, nunc et in hora mortis nostrae. Amen

Fatima Prayer—"O My Jesus, forgive us our sins, save us from the fires of hell; lead all souls to Heaven, especially those who are in most need of thy mercy.

O MI IESU, dimitte nobis debita nostra, libera nos ab igne inferni, conduc in caelum omnes animas, praesertim illas quae maxime indigent misericordia tua.

Prayer of Praise—"Glory to the Father, and to the Son, and to the Holy Spirit; as it was in the beginning, is now, and will be for ever. Amen."

Gloria Patre, et filiot, et Spirictu Sancoi, Sicut erat in principio, et nunc et semper, et in saecula saeculorum.. Amen.

Apostles' Creed—"I believe in God, the Father almighty, creator of heaven and earth. I believe in Jesus Christ, his only Son, our Lord. He was conceived by the power of the Holy Spirit and born of the Virgin Mary. He suffered under Pontius Pilate, was crucified, died, and was buried. He descended to the dead. On the third day he rose again. He ascended into heaven, and is seated at the right hand of the Father. He will come again to judge the living and the dead. I believe in the Holy Spirit, the Holy Catholic Church, the communion of saints, the forgiveness of sins, the resurrection of the body, and the life everlasting. Amen."

Credo in unum Deum: Patrem omnipotentem, factorem coeli et terrae, visibilium omnium et invisibilium. Et in unum Dominum Jesum Christum, Filium Dei unigentium. Et ex Patre natum ante omnia saecula. Deum de Deo, lumen de lumine, Deum verum de Deo vero. Genitum non factum,, consubstantialem, Patri, per quem omia facta sunt. Qui propter nos hominess, et proter nostam salutem descenmdit de coelis. Et incarnates est de Spiritu Sancto ex Maria Virgine; ET HOMO FACTUS EST. Crucifixus etiam pro nobis sub Pontio Pilato, passus, et sepiltus est. Et resurrexit tertia die, secundum Scrpturas. Et ascendit in coelum; sedet ad dexteram Patris. Et iterum venutus est cum Gloria, judicare vivos et mortuos; cujus regni non erit finis. Et in Spiritum Sanctum, Dominum et vivficantem, qui ex Patre Filioque procedit. Qui cum Patre et Filio simul adoratur et congloriofactur; qui locutus est per Prophetas. Et unam sanctam Catholicam et Apostolican Ecclesiam. Confiteor unum Baptisma in remissionem peccaorum. Et exspecto resurrectionem mortuorum et vitam venture saeculi. Amen

The Rosary as we know it today started to take its final shape in the fifteenth century. In 1483, a Dominican composed a Rosary booklet called Our Dear Lady's Psalter. It had a Rosary of 15 decades with 15 mysteries, all of which except the last two are what we have today. In 1569, Pope Pius V officially approved the 15 decade form of the Rosary we have today, and in 1573 the same Pope instituted the Feast of the Rosary in thanksgiving for the victory at the battle of Lepanto by Christians over Moslem invaders in which the Rosary played an important part.

It should be noted that while the decades and mysteries have been standardized since the time of Pope St. Pius V, the beginning and ending prayers vary with time and place. In the United States, for example, the Rosary begins with the recitation of the Creed and ends with the Salve Regina and concluding prayer (Deus, cuius Unigenitus). Another form, as practiced in Rome, begins with the "Domine, labia mea aperies", which is the starting prayer of the Hours, omits the Creed, and ends with the Litany of Loreto. Various other prayers, such as the Sub tuum praesidium have been employed as well. The prayers most often associated with the Rosary have been included here.

The most recent development in the form of Rosary occurred with the publication of Pope John Paul II's Rosarium Virginis Mariae. In it the Holy Father has added a new set of mysteries, the Luminous Mysteries, which focus on Christ's public ministry from the time of His Baptism until His Passion. Traditionally the Joyful mysteries are recited on Mondays and Thursdays, the Sorrowful mysteries are recited on Tuesdays and Fridays, and the Glorious Mysteries are recited on Wednesdays, Saturdays and Sundays. With the addition of the Luminous Mysteries, Pope John Paul II proposes that the Joyful mysteries be recited on Mondays and Saturdays, the Luminous Mysteries be recited on Thursdays, the Sorrowful mysteries are recited on Tuesdays and Fridays, and the Glorious Mysteries are recited on Wednesdays and Sundays.

Illustration # 21

Begin by making the Sign of the Cross (touch forehead, chest, left shoulder then right shoulder) saying "In the name of the Father, the Son and the Holy Ghost .

Then recite the Apostles' Creed at the crucifix, pray one Our Father first bead, one Hail Mary at each of the next three beads, and one Glory to the Father (also known as the Prayer of Praise) at the last bead on the small chain. Then recall and contemplate the first mystery, pray one Our Father before proceeding to the longer chain. Continue around as shown above, ending with "Hail Holy Queen" at the juncture.

The mysteries of the rosary are scenes from the life of Jesus and Mary. By meditating on these sublime truths, Catholics come to a better understanding of their faith: the Incarnation of the Lord, the Redemption, and the Christian life—present and future. Each mystery is followed by an aspect of your life (in parenthesis) to be contemplated and compared to the life of Christ.

The Joyful Mysteries

The messenger of God announces to Mary that she is to be the Mother of God. (Humility)

Mary visits and helps her cousin Elizabeth. (Love of Neighbor)

Mary gives birth to Jesus in a stable in Bethlehem. (Spirit of Poverty)

Jesus is presented in the Temple. (Obedience to God's Will)

Jesus is found in the Temple. (Fidelity to Vocation)

The Sorrowful Mysteries

Jesus undergoes his agony in the Garden of Gethsemane. (Spirit of Prayer)

Jesus is scourged at the pillar. (Modesty and purity)

Jesus is crowned with thorns. (Courage)

Jesus carries the cross to Calvary. (Patience in Suffering)

Jesus dies on the cross for our sins. (Self-denial)

The Glorious Mysteries

Jesus rises from the dead. (Faith)

Jesus ascends into heaven. (Hope)

The Holy Spirit comes to the apostles and the Blessed Mother. (Wisdom, Love, Zeal, Fortitude

The Mother of Jesus is taken into heaven. (Eternal Happiness)

Mary is crowned queen of heaven and earth. (Devotion to Mary and Final Perseverance)

More Prayers

Hail, Holy Queen—"Hail, holy queen, mother of mercy, our life, our sweetness, and our hope. To you we cry, poor banished children of Eve; to you wee send up our sighs, mourning and weeping n this valley of tears. Turn then, O most gracious advocate, your eyes of mercy toward us, and after this our exile, show unto us the blessed fruit of your womb, Jesus. O clement, O loving, O sweet virgin Mary.   Pray for us, O Holy Mother of God That we may be made worthy of the promises of Christ.

SALVE, Regina, mater misericordiae, vita, dulcedo, et spes nostra, salve. Ad te clamamus exsules filii Hevae. Ad te suspiramus, gementes et flentes in hac lacrimarum valle. Eia, ergo, advocata nostra, illos tuos misericordes oculos ad nos converte. Et Iesum, benedictum fructum ventris tui, nobis post hoc exsilium ostende.O clemens, O pia, O dulcis Virgo Maria. Ora pro nobis, sancta Dei Genetrix. Ut digni efficiamur promissionibus Christi. Amen.

Act of Faith—"O LORD God, I firmly believe each and every truth which the holy Catholic Church teaches, because Thou, O God, Who art eternal truth and wisdom which can neither deceive nor be deceived, hast revealed them all. In this faith I stand to live and die. Amen."

Domine Deus, firma fide credo et confiteor omnia et singula quae sancta ecclesia Catholica proponit, quia tu, Deus, ea omnia revelasti, qui es aeterna veritas et sapientia quae nec fallere nec falli potest. In hac fide vivere et mori statuo. Amen

Act of Contrition—"My God, I am sorry for my sins with all my heart. In choosing to do wrong and failing to do good, I have sinned against you whom I should love above all things. I firmly intend, with your help to do penance, to sin no more, and to avoid whatever leads me to sin. Our Savior Jesus Christ suffered and died for us. In his name my God, have mercy Amen." or "O my God, I am sorry for my sins because I have offended you. I know I should love you above all things. Help me to do penance, to do better, and to avoid anything that might lead me to sin. Amen."

DEUS meus, ex toto corde paenitet me omnium meorum peccatorum, eaque detestor, quia peccando, non solum poenas a Te iuste statutas promeritus sum, sed praesertim quia offendi Te, summum bonum, ac dignum qui super omnia diligaris. Ideo firmiter propono, adiuvante gratia Tua, de cetero me non peccaturum peccandique occasiones proximas fugiturum. Amen.

Act of Hope - " O LORD God, through Thy grace I hope to obtain remission of all my sins and after this life eternal happiness, for Thou hast promised, Who art all powerful, faithful, kind, and merciful. In this hope I stand to live and die. Amen."

Domine Deus, spero per gratiam tuam remissionem omnium peccatorum, et post hanc vitam aeternam felicitatem me esse consecuturum: quia tu promisisti, qui es infinite potens, fidelis, benignus, et misericors. In hac spe vivere et mori statuo. Amen.

Act of Love -"O LORD God, I love Thee above all things on account of Thee, because Thou art the highest, infinite and most perfect good, worthy of all love. In this love I stand to live and die. Amen."

DOMINE Deus, amo te super omnia proximum meum propter te, quia tu es summum, infinitum, et perfectissimum bonum, omni dilectione dignum. In hac caritate vivere et mori statuo. Amen.

Prayer for a Deceased Man - Incline Thine ear, O Lord, unto our prayers, wherein we humbly pray Thee to show Thy mercy upon the soul of Thy servant N., whom Thou hast commanded to pass out of this world, that Thou wouldst place him in the region of peace and light, and bid him be a partaker with Thy Saints. Through Christ our Lord. Amen.

Inclina, Domine, aurem tuam ad preces nostras, quibus misericordiam tuam supplices deprecamur, ut animam famuli tui N., quam de hoc saeculo migrare iussisti, in pacis ac lucis regione constituas et Sanctorum tuorum iubeas esse consortem. Per Christum Dominum nostrum. Amen.

Prayer for a Deceased Woman – We beseech Thee, O Lord, according to Thy loving-kindness, have mercy upon the soul of Thy handmaiden N., and now that she is set free from the defilements of this mortal flesh, restore her to her heritage of everlasting salvation. Through Christ our Lord. Amen.

Quaesumus, Domine, pro tua pietate miserere animae famulae tuae N., et a contagiis mortalitatis exutam, in aeternae salvationis partem restitue. Per Christum Dominum nostrum. Amen.

Prayer for the Dead: Let us pray for the faithful departed: Eternal rest grant unto them, O Lord, and may perpetual light shine upon them. May they rest in peace: Amen.

Oremus pro fidelibus defunctis: Requiem aeternam dona eis, Domine, et lux perpetua luceat eis. Requiescant in pace: Amen.

Blessing Before Meals - BLESS us, O Lord, and these Thy gifts which we are about to receive from Thy bounty, through Christ our Lord. Amen.

BENEDIC, Domine, nos et haec tua dona quae de tua largitate sumus sumpturi. Per Christum Dominum nostrum. Amen.

Bessing After Meals - We give Thee thanks, almighty God, for all Thy benefits, who livest and reignest for ever and ever. Amen.

Agimus tibi gratias, omnipotens Deus, pro universis beneficiis tuis, qui vivis et regnas in saecula saeculorum. Amen.

Some phrases useful in Latin. English version follows.

Per omnia saecula saeclorum. Amen - World without end. Amen.

Dominus vobiscum - The Lord be with you

Et cum spritu tuo - And with thy spirit

Sursum corda ad Dominum - Let us lift up our hearts to the Lord

Gratias agamus Domino Deo nostra - Let us give thanks to the Lord our God

Divinum auxilium maneat simper nobiscum - May the divine help remain always with us.

Miserere nostril, Domine - Have mercy on us O Lord

Dominus det nobis suam paceum Et vitam aeternam, Amen - The Lord grant us his peace and life everlasting, Amen

Deo gratius - Thanks be to God

Noctem quietam et finem perfectum concedat nobis Dominus omnipotens, Amen - The Lord God almighty grant us a quiet night and a perfect end, Amen

Dominus memor guit nodtri rt nrnrfixit nobis - The Lord hath been mindful of us and hath blessed us.

Sit Nomen Domini bebetictum in saecula - Let the name of the Lord be blessed for ever more.

Ormeus - Let us pray

Humiliate capita vestra Deo. - Bow down your heads before God.

A very valuable tool in studying Catholic prayers in Latin woild be old Missals. These have Latin and English versions of mass and are useful in locating useful prayers for any situation.

Chapter 6

Civil War Medicine

In this chapter we will cover nursing practices, surgical techniques and instruments, the care of wounds, medicines, and the creation of wounds for display and surgical scenarios.

Before we actually begin the serious stuff, I want to remind you that the more you read the more you will know. However, no one knows everything about the Civil War, Medicine of the Era, Attire, or even Mannerisms. We have a lot of written history, diaries and family histories to help us. However, remember everyone is capable of human error. We sometimes make snap judgments on people we have never met nor conversed with. As far as I know, none of us has actually conversed with someone from the Civil War, nor have we lived in the Era. There will be exceptions to everything people say about the Era. And that includes myself.

The medical training manual for Sister-nurses; "The Nursing Sister—a Manual for Candidates and Novices of Hospital Communities". was prepared by St John's Hospital Training School in Springfield, Illinois. Although written after the Civil War, it has all the training the Sisters had just prior to and during the Civil War encased in one easy to read book. Prior to it's publication in the late 1800's, teaching was most often done by route learning and on-the-job training in hospitals with other Sisters.

The original manual was printed by H. W. Rokker Co. in Springfield, IL However a reprint is in the works and may be available soon. The book is in a question and answer format. Here are some excerpts:

Q. What is the first thing to be shown in bandaging instruction?

    A. How to roll a bandage by hand.

Q. How is it done?

    A. It is taken into the right hand, the end of the strips is folded over upon itself, until you have a little roll stiff enough to keep in shape.

Q. What is the most common way of introducing medicine into the body?

    A . Through the mucous membrane, generally the stomach.

Q. In what form are medicines brought into the stomach?

    A. In various forms of pills, powders, tablets and solutions.

Q. What is sometimes given to hysterical patients?

    A An injection of water.

Q. What should be done before any medicine is given?

    A. Carefully read the label before measuring the dose and again afterward.In pouring keep the label on the upper side to avoid defacing it. Always shake the bottle before opening it; this is often important and always harmless. Never leave the bottle uncorked longer than necessary.

Q. How does fever generally announce itself?

A With a chill or a long continued chilly sensation and the bodily temperature rises.

Q. Which is the principle characteristic of typhoid fever?

A Ulceration of the bowels

Q. Which are the symptoms?

A Restless sleep, mental disquietude, dizziness, pain in different parts of the body, hot dry skin, and slight nose bleed. Sometimes nausea, slight diarrhea, and general ill feeling.

The entire book reads this way and covers everything from the qualifications needed in a Nursing Sister to how to set up hospital rooms, basic skills of nursing, symptoms of illness, how to apply or give prescribed treatments, what to report immediately to the doctor, surgical techniques and instrument care, how to deal with emergencies, fractures and dislocations and anatomy of the human body. For a training manual of that era it is quite comprehensive.

Unfortunately, I cannot begin to give you all of that information in this book and urge you to study these things on your own so as to broaden your own knowledge base. A reproduction of this work is currently being explored.

It is important to note that historically during this era, women were not allowed to work as "nurses". Men were the nurses, especially in Government run or Military run hospitals. Civilian doctors would take on newly trained doctors fresh out of school and those doctors would serve a portion of their apprenticeship doing nursing work to gain some of their skills..

That is not to say, of course, that there were not exceptions to this rule. There were many women in the United States who did follow the call of medicine at home. Many herbal remedies and home brewed medicines were handed down from one generation to the next. Practices such as these were learned at the mother or grandmother's side as she prepared medications and tended family members that were unlucky enough to fall ill.

Other than this, formal training in medicine was generally denied to women in the United States. Europe, however, was not so limited. Nursing collages had sprung up in numerous European countries and allowed enrollment of women in limited numbers.

Nursing colleges in Europe offered unique opportunities for their students to train in a variety of settings. Their training included 12 hours of intense on the job training seven days a week for 3 years under instruction of the head nurse at each facility and the surgeons in charge of the patients.

By this time, every woman who entered a convent in Europe, received training in these nursing colleges as part of their comprehensive studies. These studies were further enhanced by field work at bedlam mental hospital, debtors prisons, work houses, and battlefield hospitals.

As Europe was always in a state of chaos, many of the very skilled Sisters were often sent to battle fronts where their education would continue. They honed skills in triage techniques (called sorting the wounded), emergency first aide (called staunching wounds), and the best drug administration techniques. Often these Sisters would be requested to help in the surgical theaters where they assisted surgeons in the latest of surgical practices. They worked side by side with the surgeons and assistant surgeons during their rounds in makeshift hospitals, tented wards and established hospitals.

When the United States began to receive it's first Sisters as missionaries in the mid-1700's, it was these highly skilled women that were Europe's gifts to America. When the first shot of the Civil War was fired, it was these women who were best prepared for the onslaught of chaotic carnage that ensued.

By 1862, nursing Sisters were much in demand. Many of the convents on the east coast and mid-west sent Sisters to work with governmental and army medical staff from the start of the conflict to the bitter end. The first nursing college, Bellvue Hospital in New yok City, produced its first graduate in 1872. Far too, late for the Civil War.

Medical statistics are widely available in many books and tell their own gruesome tales. A general understanding of what this meant to the medical staff caring for the ill and wounded is a shocking and heart rendering tale best left to the imagination. We must understand the ability of human nature to set aside the big picture in order to attend the daily details immediately before them. That is how the Sisters, surgeons and stewards would deal with the horrors before them. Union statistics alone showed that half a million soldiers were treated for injuries, six million were treated for serious diseases, 50,000 amputations were performed and all by 4,000 acting surgeons that eventually served in the Union army. This means that each surgeon cared for approximately 1,638 patients during the four year war. This did not include the other duties demanded of the surgeons in the field such as dentistry, sick call for minor illnesses, inspections of camp followers for diseases, latrines and camp kitchens for sanitary measures, reports and follow-up paperwork that had to be completed, and of course, that minor detail of sleep.

Was it any wonder then that the Sisters were sought after for their ability to make decisions and follow orders correctly? Add that to the fact that most Sisters were bi-lingual at the very least (some knew up to five different languages!) and could act as interpreters for the immigrant soldiers that had flooded the nation's army.

Surgical Techniques

It wasn't until four months after the Civil War ended in 1865, that Joseph Lister, having become familiar with microbiology, began combining the idea of infectious diseases with wound contamination. This resultied in an almost manic obsession of washing hands and surgical instruments in a dilute solution of carbolic acid. It was twelve years after that beginning that aseptic techniques finally caught hold in the medical communities of the United States—far too late to help the patients during the American Civil War.

Why am I telling you this? Because many of our portrayals fall into the trap of modern day thinking. One such portrayal, is that surgical and medical instruments must have been washed before each and every patient. That is common sense, right?   NO!

During the Victorian era, Doctors and surgeons would not have known the germ theory of thought. It hadn't been invented. The only reason to wash instruments was to prevent their slipping out of the wielder's hands during a series of multiples surgeries, or to clean them before putting them away to prevent rust! They also used dirty sponges if clean ones were unavailable, reused bandages and linens, bedding straw was infrequently changed and utensils were frequently shared between patients.

Prior to any surgical theater, familiarize yourself with your surgeon and the instruments available to you and where they are kept.. Ask the surgeon his preference in tools for common procedures. This not only impresses the surgeon for whom you will be working with your professionalism (he may ask you to come work with him again) but also keeps you from making huge mistakes in front of the civilian audience. Little mistakes are more tolerable as the audience is too entranced to notice (unless you keep making the same one and the surgeon points out the inadequacy). It's the big mistakes like handing the surgeon a saw when he only needs a scalpel. The audience is likely to focus on that instead of the surgical technique before them.

Each surgeon will have special techniques and procedures that he likes to show case. Be familiar with the ones your surgeons use. Get to know their instrument boxes and supply boxes and know what is available so you can hand items to them when they are needed or requested quickly and efficiently.

Field Tourniquet (1) was most often used for quick use. The Screw type tourniquet (2) was most used in hospital surgeries.

1

2

Probes shown below were used to locate bullets buried in wounds.

3

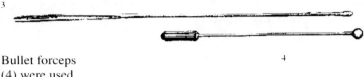

Bullet forceps (4) were used to remove bullets and came in various sizes and types.

4

Bone saws (5) also came in a variety of shapes and sizes

5

Amputation knife (6) is a single edged blade as opposed to the smaller double edged blade of the Catlin knife(7). Both were used during amputations.

6

7

Tenaculum (8) is used to hook arteries and pull them out for the surgeon to tie off to prevent hemorrhaging (9).
Scalpels (right) come in many more shapes and sizes than shown here and each has a specific use.

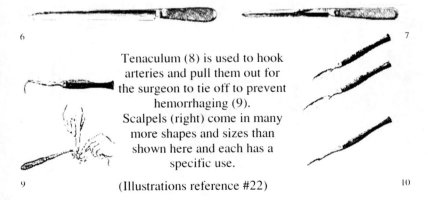

9

(Illustrations reference #22)

10

95

Linen Tissue Puller (right) is used to retract muscle and tissue to allow surgeon access to bone for amputation. Approximately 12" x 24" the cloth is cut with three tails to slip between both bones in this example. The two tail cloth (below-right) is used for single bone amputations. The competent surgeon (below) can complete an amputation in under 6 minutes.

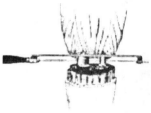

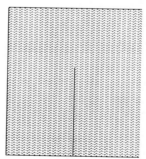

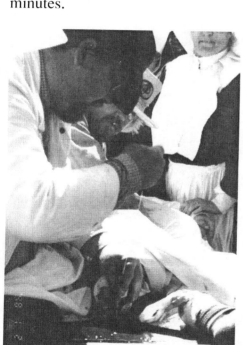

(Illustration Refrence #23 & 24)

Amputations

Amputations are among the most gruesome and the most requested of surgeries. They are also the most difficult to prepare for and do by the medical team and require precision team work to carry them off. It is often the surgical nurse that is able to make sure the surgeon looks good in this particular technique. This is one that you and your surgeon will have to work together and practice before hand. The following is an equipment list in order of use:

Tourniquet: Used to stem the flow of blood

Long Catling   : Double sided and pointed soft tissue knife used to cut skin flaps and cut through muscle and tissue.

Small sharp instrument of surgeon's choice: Used to pop blood and puss bags to enhance impression of actual surgery.

Tissue pullers (cloth or metal):   Used to pull back tissues so as to allow surgeon to saw through bone without further damaging tissues and muscles.

Bone Saw: To cut through bone.

Tenaculum: Used to hook arteries and make them available to tie off to prevent hemorrhaging in wound.

Suturing material: Needle and silk thread or horse hair that has been boiled to make pliable.

Bandages: Created from cotton gauze material or ripping old sheets or muslin in 3" x 3 yard strips then rolled.

Also you may find   a flask and sponge useful for administering an anesthetic such as ether.

Preparation:

Fake leg or arm should be cut in area above the wound area created by moulage. On each end create two holes that correspond with each other approximately 1" deep. Cut 5" dowel rods the circumference of the holes these need to seat well enough to create at least a 3" gap between upper and lower limb parts.. These will create your "bones."

Drill a third hole in the upper portion of a smaller circumference that a plastic tube from an enema bag will travel through. This hole needs to go all the way through the prosthetic to allow bag to be hidden in upper area while tubing travels through hole down to gap between portions. The bag will hold blood that can be forced through the plastic "artery" by having the assistant or the surgical nurse squeeze the bag in pulsating pressures. This step can be eliminated if you find a squirting artery is too graphic for your audience.

The next step is to create the muscle tissue. Two 1 1/2" thick pieces of steak cut to size of limb circumference should do well. The cheaper the cut the better. Place the steaks on top of each other and cut an "X" where the dowel rods will insert through them. Between the two pieces of steak you can place blood or pus bags and your plastic artery should also be pushed through the top piece of steak so blood will squirt from meat area. On the end of the tube place a balloon with the round part cut off so that a tenaculum can be used to pull this softer part out of steak to be tied off with suture material. Cover the entire gap with either pig or chicken skin tied at each end with string tightly so skin will not slip.

The limb, now prepared for the presentation should be used quickly. The tricky part is to have it hidden under the table so that it can be placed and held by stewards while surgery is being undertaken by surgeons. The patient should be covered with a sheet or blanket to disguise the fact that he has the leg or arm bent out of the way and the fake limb is being held in place by assistants or strapped in place at the bend of elbow or knee. When draping the patient the blanket can be held up momentarily to block the view of observers while the artificial limb is being lifted into place.

Procedure:

If a cloth tissue puller is to be used it should be placed under leg first so that the ends can be pulled through the "bone" structure to hold the muscle out of the way for the capital saw to be used later. Tourniquet should be applied next to "stop bleeding"

With a long catlin cut skin close to the edge of lower cut of artificial limb all the way around so that it separates. If necessary use a sharp scalpel to aid in this procedure.

Peel back skin as if peeling off a sock. Run catlin between the two pieces of steak as if cutting through muscle, puncturing any balloons of blood or puss as you go. Any not punctured in this manner should be either punctured with sharp instrument of choice or discreetly removed.

With tissue pullers hold back upper steak piece to expose the dowel rod "bones". A capital saw is then used to cut through the dowel rods.

Release tissue pullers next. If you have the fake artery set up ready your assistant should now begin to apply alternating pressure to create squirts of blood. Tell assistant to tighten the tourniquet. This will be the signal for him to stop the pressure. Using a tenaculum hook the balloon part of the "artery" and gently pull out into view and tie closed with suture material. Have assistant release tourniquet to "test the artery for leaks.

Once the lower part of the limb is disposed of out the sight of the audience you can begin to fold over the skin and suture it closed in a flap shape. Stewards or nurses should then bandage the "stump"

As I stated before, this is one procedure that will need practice with surgeon, assistants and surgical nurses together in precision teamwork.

Bullet Extractions

This procedure is one of the most used and simplest to prepare for. However care must be given to placement of the wound and placement of the patient on the table so as to give the surgeon maximum manipulation room while giving observers the opportunity to see the procedure being done.

Instruments:

Tourniquet: Used to stem the flow of blood

Bullet probe: to locate foreign matter

Small sharp instrument of surgeon's choice: Use to pop blood and puss bags to enhance impression of actual surgery.

Tissue pullers (cloth or metal):   Used to pull back tissues so as to allow surgeon better access to inside of the wound

Scalpel: To enlarge wound or to lance blood bags or puss bags

Billet forceps: Used to remove bullets, fragments and ripped tissue from wound.

Suturing material : Needle and silk thread or horse hair that has been boiled to make pliable.

Bandages: Created from cotton gauze material or ripping old sheets or muslin in 3" x 3 yard strips then rolled.

Also you may find a flask and sponge useful for administering an anesthetic such as ether.

Preparation: The quick on the spot method of preparation involves simply wrapping the area with bandaging and inserting into the folds blood and puss bags, ripped tissues (chicken liver makes excellent ripped tissues), smashed lead bullets, bone fragments or other materials.

Preperation:

Advanced preparation can be a prepared bandage with a sponge insert moulaged to look like a wound with an opening. The sponge is glued to the bandage around the outer edge so that items can be placed into the split in the sponge and hidden in the resulting pocket under the sponge. Many have also sewn a piece of plastic inside the bandage under the sponge to protect uniforms. Make the ends of the bandages long enough to wrap several time to hide the edges of the sponge and tie it in a slip not fashion for easy release. I usually make several of these in different sizes because patient are different sizes and you may need extra length for larger patients.

Procedure:

A tourniquet should be placed above the wound loosely. A probe is then used to locate the bullet and fragments. Often the surgeon may find the bullet probe useless and use his fingers instead. A scalpel may be used to enlarge wound for better access or to clear debris and puncture blood and puss bags.

Tissue pullers may be used if available to the assistant to hold tissue apart for surgeon so he can see better into the wound. Bullet forceps are then used to remove matter in the wound including the bullet.

When available a glass irrigator can be used to clear small debris from wound. In larger wounds sponges created from lint tied in tiny squares of gauze can be used and talc to simulate opiate type powders as pain killers sprinkled into the wound.

Wound is then sutured by the surgeon and the steward can then bandage the patient and remove him from surgical table.

Head Wounds

Head wounds were fairly common and frequently mishandled. For our purposes simple is better and will take the least preparations and equipment.

Instruments:

Bullet probe: to locate foreign matter

Small sharp instrument of surgeon's choice: Use to pop blood and puss bags to enhance impression of actual surgery.

Suture material and thread: To suture open wound

Sponges: lint or cotton ball in small bundle wrapped in a small square of gauze and tied with thread. These are moistened and used to pack wounds.

Scissors: to cut sutures

Bandages: To wrap head and apply pressure.

Preparation:

Realistically it is rather impossible for the beginning surgeon to find and afford a trephaning set that was used to relieve pressure on the brain. For our purposes the head wound will be entirely superficial in nature but, the scenario can run that the patient is suffering from "trauma related mentation" (a blow to the head that rattles the brain causing slowness and inability to think clearly). Wrap the head area and place in the bandage folds a small packet of blood. Smear a little fake blood on outside of bandage as well. Instruct your patient to appear glassy-eyed and dazed.

Procedure:
A bullet probe or finger can be used to locate any debris to be cleaned out. The sharp instrument can be used under the pretext of cleansing out some larger debris to puncture blood bag. Suture wound closed or pack with sponges. Bandage as usual for head wound. If a priest is available he can use this opportunity to converse with patient. If not assign a nurse to the patient for care reminding her/him to watch carefully for signs of serious mental changes.

Gut Wounds

These wounds were frequently ignored until very last since they were the least understood and had the poorest recovery rate. Usually these patients were left under a shady tree until the surgeon had dealt with all the other injuries. If the surgeon plans on doing surgery he will need a soft tissue tray that includes the following:

Instruments:
Bullet probe: used to find bullets or debris.
Small sharp instrument of surgeon's choice: Use to pop blood and puss bags to enhance impression of actual surgery.
Tissue pullers (cloth or metal): Used to pull back tissues so as to allow surgeon better access to inside of the wound
Scalpel: To enlarge wound or to lance blood bags or puss bags
Billet forceps: Used to remove bullets, fragments and ripped tissue from wound.
Suture material: Needle and silk thread or horse hair that has been boiled to make pliable.
Also you may find a flask and sponge useful for administering an anesthetic such as ether.
Bandages: Created from cotton gauze material or ripping old sheets or muslin in 3" x 3 yard strips then rolled.
Sponges: Pieces of lint or cotton balls in gauze and tied with thread. They are packed into wounds to absorb blood, puss and other fluids to aid in healing wounds left open to air (particularly large wounds.

Preparation:
Gut wounds may fit under the shirt of the patient. Wrap torso with large bandages. Insert one or more of the following: large sausage link, long balloon filled with items to recreate stomach contents, blood and pus bags, bullet and/or debris. Mixing a little pepper in with wound contents to represent gun powder works well. Patient should be instructed to expect to

die on surgical table. Having available crushed Alka-Seltzer tablet mixed with powdered sweetened cherry drink mix to place in mouth to create bloody foam as saliva hits it is a fun way to create a death scene. Have patient spit it out as it foams so as not to choke on it and to create the maximum affect.

Procedure:

Plan on the surgeon grumbling or shouting about the waste of valuable time on a patient that is going to die anyway. Try softening his disposition by praising his skills and ability to work miracles. Surgeon may use either bullet probe or fingers to locate bullets and debris. A bullet forceps is used to remove the debris and the bullet carefully working around simulated bowel. These may also be punctured allowing contents to spill out. If this happens the patient should be given a sip of water with the Alka-Seltzer powder for a death scene.

The surgeon may or may not wash out the wound before packing with sponges and loose suturing the wound closed (supposing the patient has survived without the death scene).

More Helpful Items to Note

Clear latex balloons are available at party supply stores and come I packages of 50 or 100. These are wonderful for either blood or puss and with a little care when empty can simulate tissue for easy removal and disposal in front of observers. To prepare them first stretch them and blow them up let out most of the air and insert the nozzle of you bottle of fake blood and squeeze in needed blood. Remove nozzle carefully and tie off. The little bit of air in the balloon puts pressure in so that blood will squirt out as balloon is punctured. The same can be done with puss. If maggots are needed insert dry rice first before blowing up and filling. Be sure to trim off edge of tail so it is not easily recognizable as a balloon.

Blood can be made a variety of ways. Corn syrup colored with children's red finger paint is ok or blue laundry soap with finger paints is also good. Finger paints are my favorite instead of food dye because it is non-toxic and washes out of most fabrics.

Puss is often made with vanilla pudding diluted slightly.

Maggots can be simulated with dry rice.

Pepper sprinkled in wound simulates gun powder.

Chapter 7

Information

After all the attention dies down and the visitors go home, I like to sit and reflect on the day's events. Sometimes I make notes about things I would change and other times I reflect on visitor's reactions to my persona.

There have been many times when visitors have had to ask if I was a real Nun or not. To me, this type of reaction tells me that I'm doing things right. This is the best compliment one can get.

Catholics that have had the influence of the Sisters in their lives know better than most how different each is in personality, yet so alike in demeanor. These people are a veritable well spring of information.

Relax in your new role. Let it expand around you a create that aura that seems to go with being a Sister. Be deliberate in your actions.

Perhaps one day I shall meet you at a reenactment and we'll exchange stories and information!

May the light guide your footsteps along the path,
Kelsey

Ilustration References

Illustration 1: The Sister Bride (cover) CDV - Private Collection of Kelsey Jones.

Illustration 2: Pope Pius IX, Print – Private Collection of Kelsey Jones.

Illustration 3: Nursing Daughter of Charity, Print - Private Collection of Kelsey Jones.

Illustration 4: A Nun's Cell, CDV - Private Collection of Kelsey Jones.

Illustration 5: Civil War Priest, CDV - Private Collection of Kelsey Jones.

Illustration 6: Daughters of Charity – from the "Guide to Catholic Sisterhoods in the United States", 1955

Illustration 7: Sisters of Mercy – from the "Guide to Catholic Sisterhoods in the United States", 1955

Illustration 8: Sisters of the Holy Cross – from the "Guide to Catholic Sisterhoods in the United States", 1955

Illustration 9: Sisters of Charity, Cincinatti – from the "Guide to Catholic Sisterhoods in the United States", 1955

Illustration 10: Sisters of Charity, New York – from the "Guide to Catholic Sisterhoods in the United States", 1955

Illustration 11: Sisters of Charity, Nazareth – from the "Guide to Catholic Sisterhoods in the United States", 1955

Illustration 12: Sister of the Poor of St. Francis – from the "Guide to Catholic Sisterhoods in the United States", 1955

Illustration 13: Sisters of St. Dominic, Springfield, KY – from the "Guide to Catholic Sisterhoods in the United States", 1955

Illustration 14: Sisters of St. Dominic, Memphis, TN – from the "Guide to Catholic Sisterhoods in the United States", 1955

Illustration 15: Sisters of St. Joseph – from the "Guide to Catholic Sisterhoods in the United States", 1955

Illustration 16: Sisters of Charity of Our lady of Mercy – from the "Guide to Catholic Sisterhoods in the United States", 1955

Illustration 17: Sisters of Providence – from the "Guide to Catholic Sisterhoods in the United States", 1955

Illustration 18: Sisters of Our Lady of Mount Carmel – from the "Guide to Catholic Sisterhoods in the United States", 1955

Illustration 19: Sisters of St. Ursula – from the "Guide to Catholic Sisterhoods in the United States", 1955

Illustration 20: Sisters of St. Brigid – CDV, Private collection of Kelsey Jones

Illustration 21: Rosary – electronic scan

Illustration 22 &23: Surgical Instruments – Drawings "Civil War Medicine",1998

Illustration 24: Surgical Amputation – photo, Private collection of Kelsey Jones

Glossary

Abbess – Woman in charge of an abbey (a place for religious study and work).

Bandeau – the cap like devide that supports the veil.

Barter – a system of trading surplusgoods or services for needed goods and services.

Beleaguered – harrassed, abused.

Benedictine – those following the doctrine of St. Benedictine.

Bloomers – period under-garment worn like todays underpants.

Burgh – town

Candidacy – the role of being a candidate, a period in which a woman spends her time in a cloister before starting her education as a nun.

Canonical hours – periods of prayers decreed by the church to be followed by sequestered religious groups.

Chancellor – the chief minister of state or head of a university.

Chancellorship – one who holds the office of chancellor.

Cardinal – a high religious office

Chatelaines – a person in charge of the duties of household servents. May or may not be the mistress of the estate.

Chemise – Period undergarment worn like a slip of today.

Cloister – compound of buildings to which religious persons live away from the influence of the outside community.

Coffers – a place where money is kept as in a bank account or money box.

Coif – the head covering worn beneath the veil and bandeau.

Community (religious) – a term indicating a single group of women working together with a Mother Superior or Sister Superior as director. These Communities are usually part of a greater whole called a Religious Order.

Conical – the months 6 through 18, a time of the most rigourous study and most vigourous training.

Cricifix – differing from a cross in that it has the figure of Christ upon it

Daughters of Charity – see page 44

Dissolution – disbanding of, dissolving a group.

Divine Institution – work that furthers the interest of God and maintains the business of running a religious compound or church.

Divine Office – a group of prayers the Catholic Church uses to help direct the mind to worship.

Doctrine – a set of religious beliefs.

Dowery – that which a woman takes to a marriage (or in this case to a religious community) consisting of money or land and personal property.

Ecclesiastic – a clergy, relating to church matters as an institution.

Endowed colleges – Colleges that received financial support from outside sources (as a monarch).

Episcopal See – authority and jurisdiction of a bishop.

Frippery – laces and finery.

Feudal tenure – the right to own property directly related to the ability to hold and defend it.

Genteel – refering to the upper class as apposed to working class.

Guimpe – the large collar that makes up part of the Sisters' habit.

Habit – technically the dress portion of the Sisters' uniform. Also used as a general term for the entire ensamble of the uniform.

Ire – anger

Mistress of Novices – a Sister who is in charge of the education, housing and training of Postulates and Novices.

Modesty slip – period undergarment worn to prevent the accidental showing of leg.

Modicum – a moderate amount of…(anything)

Monestary – a house reserved for the use of monks or nuns for the purpose of sequestering them from society.

Monastic – solitary or sequestered life style of religious centers.

Monasticism – refering to the act of creating a group of men or women under vows to further religious study and work in a sequestered area for religious persons.

Monk – a male that has entered a monastic center for religious studies and has taken a vow of poverty, chastity and obedience.

Mother Superior – an official head of an order usually selected by a group of her peers and approved by a Bishop.

Novice – a person in the second period (months 6 through 18) of education for religious life within an Order.

Novitiate – a separate building or area within the main house of a religious Community designed to house postulates and novices.

Nun – a woman under solemn vows of poverty, chastity and obedience to God. Usually this also means they are cloistered. While this term is not technically interchangeable with the word Sister, lay persons not of Catholic faith have been known to use this term to indicate all women in monastic life.

Order – a term used to indicate that several communities are working together as one unit usually with one Mother superior as over-all director and Sister Superior as individual community directors. Example: Sisters of Mercy have approximately 30 communities working together under one name.

Penance – a duty or series of prayers and contemplations given to one who has erred and is designed to teach correct thoughts or behavior.

Prelate – a clergy of high rank (as a bishop).

Postulate – women who are at the first six months of their religious training to join a religious order.

Permanent Vows – solemn vows that are taken as a final step to becoming a permanent member of a Religious Community.

Perpetual Vows – differing from permanent vows in that they are repeated every year as long as the woman remains a member of the Religious Community.

Retinue – those persons that accompany one of high rank during travel. An example would be companions and servants.

Rosary – a grouping of beads on a rope or chain whith which Catholics keep track of prayers. (see page 87)

Sanctification – to free from sin or make holy.

Scapular – part of the Sisters' habit. Usually a straight piece of cloth that is worn over the dress portion reaching the hem of the dress. The Sisters frequently place their hands under this part of their garment when idle.

Sequestered – seperating from public influences, usually for religious purposes.

Severance – seperated from.

Simple vows – vows of poverty, chastity and obedience to God that have been taken in private and are not formally recognized by the Catholic Church.

Sister – a woman who has taken Simple vows of poverty, chastity and obedience to God. Sisters are never cloistered. This term is frequently used interchangably with the term Nun. Sister is also the title with which all Sisters and Nuns address each other.

Sisters of St. Brigid (S. S. B.) – See page 76

Sisters of St. Brigid Community – See page 76

Sisters of Charity, Cincinatti – See page 57

Sisters of Charity, Nazareth – See page 60

Sisters of Charity, New York – See page 59

Sisters of Charity of Our lady of Mercy – See page 69

Sisters of St. Dominic, Memphis, TN – See page 65

Sisters of St. Dominic, Springfield, KY – See page 63

Sisters of St. Joseph – See page 67

Sisters of the Holy Cross – See page 54

Sisters of Mercy – See page 49

Sisters of Our Lady of Mount Carmel – See page 72

Sisters of the Poor of St. Francis – See page 62

Sisters of Providence – See page 71

Sisters of St. Ursula – See page 74

Sister Superior – official head of a Community of Sisters when there are a large number of Communities within an Order. Elected by her

107

peers within the Community and approved by the Mother Superior of the Order. This allows each to have some autonomy while still being directed by a Mother Superior.

Sisters of St. Brigid Community – a group of women portraying Nuns of different eras that share information and help with training of novice reenactors.

Solemn vows – vows of poverty, chastity and obedience to God that are taken publically and are formally recognized by the Catholic Church.

Surgical Instruments – See pages 95 and 96 for illustrations.

Ticking mattress – a roughly sewn sack of heavy cloth in which is stuffed straw or feathers for sleeping on. The stuffing is usually changed every six months.

Trephaning – A tool used to open the scull to relieve pressure on the brain.

Trousseau – personal garments that are part of a woman's dowery.

Under-pinnings – a collection of period underclothes such as bloomers, chemise and modesty slip.

Vestments – robe and outer clothing (as scapular) worn by clergy for religious ceremony.

Vice-regent – administrative deputy

Vows - Vow of chastity (to never marry or have intercourse with an earthly man), poverty (to not own property of any kind) and Obedience (to do God's bidding in the form of the clergy or Mother Superior)

Women Religious – a historical term meaning any group of women gathered together for the study of religion and to further the religious work for which they formed their group. This includes Convents and other monastic societies.

List of Prayers

Web Sites to Visit:

http://www.ehistory.com/index.cfm - This site seems to be a well spring of papers and pages on Civil War Medicine.

http://home.earthlink.net/%7Ethesaurus/index.htm - Michael Martin's web site with a very comprehensive group of Catholic prayers in both English and Latin. Well worth taking a look at!

http://www.evangelist.org/archive/htm/1126civl.htm - Civil War wounded were comforted by Sisters By Masureen McGuiness. This paper is on Sister Nurses in particular.

http://www.catholicprayers.com/html/o_basic.html - A site full of Catholic Prayers.

http://www.civilwarhome.com/hospitalssurgeonsnurses.htm - A page on hospitals and surgeons.

http://www.powerweb.net/bbock/war/amputate.html - This is a page on just amputations.

http://www.civilwarhome.com/civilwarmedicineintro.htm - A site with several pages on Civil War Medicine.

http://www.geocities.com/brigidsisters/ - A Sisters of St. Brigid Community site. Information and photos.

Sisters of St. Brigid Community contacts:

Mother Superior Mary Elizabeth, S.S.B.   (Kelsey Jones)
1121 3rd St. SW; Mason City, Ia 51401   brigidsisters@yahoo.com

Sister Superior Mary Theresa, S.S.B. (Linda Gessner)
Northern Illinois group attached to 45th US Medical
1422 Howland Dr.; Joliet, IL 60431-6050   815-254-1396

Sister Mary Michaeline, S.S.B. (Kristan Martin)
North western Wisconsin group attached to 16th US Medical
2940 150th St; Fredrick, WI 54837
715-327-8302   k_m_nelson@hotmail.com

Sister Dewey (Dewey McConnville)
Iowa Group attached to 16th US Medical
RR2 Valley Dr.; Centerville, IA 52544   deweym@se-iowa.com

Sr. Mary Angela (Angela Adler)
Sisters of Charity New York Group
2975 Lincoln Ave.; Oceanside, NY 11572-3011

Sr. Mary Elizabeth RSM(OSU) (Cindy Lambert)
Sisters of Charity Louisiana Group
PO Box 247; St. Rose, LA 70087   mercynun@aol.com

Lona Morse
Sisters of Charity –Kansas group
1944 Crest Dr.; Topeka, KS 66604   phil@KScommercial.com

Olinda Bell
7594 Chablis Circle; Navarre, FL 32566-8400

Susan Covey
1038 Highland Ave.; Louisville, KY 40204-1961
Amy B. Fairweather
1101 W. Wittmore Ave.; Flint, MI 48507

Sherri George
455 Jefferson St.; Twinfalls, ID 83301

Emily Herman
2835 S. Fort Ave. #813; Springfield, MO 65807

Judee Himbaugh
26723 N. Isabella Parkway #103 ; Canyon Country, CA 91351-4892

Sr. Mary Stanislaus Murphy, RSM (Nichole Lovejoy)
3292 Lakewood Dr.; Janesville, OH 43701
adamandnichole@globalco.net

Kristen Nelson   Sr. Holy Cross group
171 Lexington Ave.; San Leandra, CA 94677   g_v_nelson@msn.com

Karen Kerkla—Nurse
PO Bx 11; Suakville, WI 53080-0011

Sr. M. Margaret, S. C. (Margaret M. Gilbert)
Sisters of Charity –Minnesota Group attached to 4th US Medical
1350 Nicollet Ave. Apt.#1016 Minneapolis, Mn. 55403-2641
612-879-8453   nurse_4thus@yahoo.com

Mother Houses to Contact:
    Sisters of St. Brigid - Sr. Theresa Carter CSB
        5118 Loma Linda Dr.; San Antonio, TX 78201
    Daughters of Charity - Bonnie Weatherly, archivist
        Provincial House Emmitsburg, Maryland 21727
        (301) 447-3121
    Sisters of St. Dominic - Rev. Mother General
        Catharine of Sienna Convent, St. Cathamine, Kentucky
    Sisters of St. Dominic - Rev. Mother Superior, 0. P.
        St. Cecilia Convent, Nashville, Tennessee.
    Sisters of St. Dominic - Mother Mary Imelda, O.P.
        Sacred Heart Convent, Springfield, Illinois
    Franciscan Sisters of the Poor –Reverend Mother Provincial, St.
        Glare Convent, Hartwell, Cincinnati, Ohio
    Sisters of Charity - Reverend Mother General
        Mount St. Joseph, Cincinnati, Ohio.
    Sisters of Charity - Reverend Mother General
        Mount St. Vincent-on-Hudson, New York 71, N. Y.
    Sisters of Charity - Mother General
        Mother House of Sisters of Charity of Nazareth, Nazareth,
        Kentucky
    Sisters of Charity - Reverend Mother Provincial
        St. Glare Convent, Hartwell, Cincinnati, Ohio.

Sisters of the Poor of St. Francis - Reverend Mother Provincial, St. Glare Convent, Hartwell, Cincinnati, 15, Ohio.

Sisters of Charity - Reverend Mother General
Mount St. Joseph, Cincinnati, Ohio.

Sisters of Charity of St. Vincent de Paul - the Reverend Mother General   Mount St. Vincent-on-Hudson, New York 71, N. Y.

Sisters of Charity of Nazareth - Mother General
Mother House of Sisters of Charity of Nazareth, Nazareth, Kentucky.

Sisters of the Holy Cross - The Mistress of Novices
St. Mary's Novitiate; Notre Dame, Indiana.

Sisters of Mercy - Convent of Our Lady of Mercy, Auburn, California; Convent of Our Lady of Mercy, 2300 Adeline Dr., Burlingame, California; St. Joseph's Convent of Mercy; 160 Farmington Ave., Hartford, Connecticut; Sacred Heart Convent Elmhurst Dr., Cedar Rapids, Iowa; St Joseph's Convent, 605 Stevens Ave., Portland , Maine; St. Gabriel's Convent of Our Lady of Mercy, 46 High St., Worcester, Massachusetts; Mt. St. Mary's Convent, 435 Union St., Manchester, New Hampshire; Motherhouse, Sisters of Mercy, State Highway No. 29 at Tirrell Rd., North Plainfield, New Jersey; New York; Convent of Mercy, 634 New Scotland Ave., Albany, New York; St. Francis Convent, Sisters of Mercy, 273 Willoughby Ave., Brooklyn 5, New York; Convent of Our Lady of Mercy, 625 Abbot Rd., Buffalo 20, New York; Motherhouse of the Sisters of Mercy, 1437 Blossom Rd., Brighton Station, Rochester, New York; Sacred Heart Convent, Belmont, North Carolina; St. Joseph's Convent, 512 W. Main St., Titusville, Pennsylvania; Motherhouse of the Sisters of Mercy, Merion, Pennsylvania; St. Mary's Convent, 3333 Fifth Ave., Pittsburgh, Pennsylvania; Vermont---Mt. St. Mary's Academy, Mansfield Ave., Burlington, Vermont;

The following belong to the Sisters of Mercy of the Union in the U.S.A.
Motherhouse---Rev. Mother General R.S.M., Villa Mercy, 9800 Kentsdale Dr., Bethesda P.O. Washington 14, D. C.; Baltimore Province---Provincial House, Holy Family Convent, Mt. Washington 9, Maryland; Chicago Province---Provincial House, 4845 Ellis Ave., Chicago 15, Illinois; Cincinnati Province---Provincial House, 2220 Victory Parkway, Cincinnati 6, Ohio; Detroit Province---Provincial

House, 8200 West Outer Drive, Detroit 19, Michigan; New
York Province---Provincial House, Wilson Park,
Tarrytown, New York; Omaha Province---Provincial
House, 3506 Hawthorne Ave., Omaha 3, Nebraska;
Providence Province---Provincial House, Manville P.O.,
Providence, Rhode Island; St. Louis Province---Provincial
House, 723 Laclede Station Rd., Webster Groves 19,
Missouri; Scranton Province---Provincial House, Villa St.
Teresa, Dallas, Pennsylvania;

Sisters of the Poor of St. Francis - Reverend Mother Provincial
St. Glare Convent, Hartwell, Cincinnati, 15, Ohio.

Sisters of Our Lady of Mount Carmel -Rev. Mother Mary Rita, 0.
Carm. Mount Carmel Motherhouse, 420 Robert E. Lee
Blvd., New Orleans, Louisiana

Sisters of St. Joseph -St. Joseph's Convent, Eoff & 14th Sts.,
Wheeling, West Virginia

Sisters of Charity of Our Lady of Mercy - Charleston, S.C.
Sisters of Providence - St. Mary of the Woods, Indiana

Ursuline Nuns - Ursuline Convent, 1316 Galveston St., Laredo,
Texas.

Barton, George. *Angels of the Battlefield*. Philadelphia, PA, 1898

Beatty, William K. and Marks, Geoffrey. *Women In White*. New York: Charles Scribner's Sons, 1972

Eckenstein, Lina. *Woman Under Monasticism*. London: Cambridge University Press, 1896

Farren, Susan. *A Call to Care*. St. Louis: Schalin Brothers Printing Company, 1996

Jolly, Ellen Ryan. *Nuns of the Battlefield*. Providence Visitor (Providence) , 1927

McCarthy, Thomas P. C.S.V.. *Guide to the Catholic Stisterhoods in the United States.* Publisher Unknown, 1955 (CD)

Maher, Sister Mary Denis. *To Bind Up the Wounds, Catholic Sister Nurses in the U.S. Civil War*. Baton Rouge, LA: Louisiana State University Press, 1989

Parente, Pascal P. S.T.D., Ph.D., J.C.B. *The Mystical Life*. London, W.C.: B Herder Book Co. 1945

Raphael, Mother Frances, O.S.D. The Daily life of a Religious. Unknown Pulisher 1914 (CD)

St. John's Hospital Training School. *The Nursing Sister, A Manual for Candidates and Novices of Hospital Communities*. Springfield, IL. 1899

Thibodeau, Richard, C.SS.R. *The Essential Catholic Handbook*. United States of America: Liguori Publications. 1978

Walsh, James J. *These Splendid Sisters*. New York: J. H. Sears and Company, Incoorporated, 1926

Wilbur, C. Keith, M.D. *Civil War Medicine, 1861-1865*. Old Syabrook, Connedticut: The Globe Pequot Press, 1998

The Author

Kelsey Jones is a retired nurse and has been Civil War reenacting since 1994 and her portrayal of a Civil War Nun in the summer of 1997. She has since established the role as a serious and highly respected part of history for the United States. The establishment of the Sisters of St. Brigid Community as an umbrella organization for women who reenact as Civil War Nuns and Sisters helped numerous women establish their own roles.

Her continued research helps to increase the field of knowledge for the reenacting and lay communities alike. She gives talks to schools on a frequent basis and continues to participate in the reenacting community. She works with numerous units in the mid-west to assist in establishing Sister groups.